KAT SCHOOL HANDBOOK

Printed in the United States of America.

> **Disclaimer:** This book is to be used for supplemental training only. It is not intended to provide any legal, medical, or professional advice, nor is it a substitute for training with a qualified Master Instructor. Techniques described in the book can result in injury to yourself or others. Everyone should practice these techniques only under qualified supervision.

www.kattaekwondo.com

Korean Academy of Taekwondo
Official School Handbook

Compiled and Edited by:

Master Bill Pottle and Master Katie Pottle

1ˢᵗ Edition – January 2005
2ⁿᵈ Edition- January 2007
3ʳᵈ Edition – January 2011
4ᵗʰ Edition – March 2018

Table of Contents

Contents

Part 1: Basics

Welcome

Welcome to the Korean Academy of Taekwondo. You are the heir to a proud tradition of hard work, competition, friendship, respect, and trust. This handbook has been compiled to help students understand more about Taekwondo at the Korean Academy and its various KAT Network programs. The handbook is divided into different sections—feel free to read all of them but at a minimum be sure to read the basics section and the chapter for your belt. In your time with us, you can look forward to testing yourself, reaching new limits, and forging lifelong bonds of friendship.

How to Use This Book

Part 1: Basics – All students and parents should read.
Part 2: Belt Curriculum – Focus on your current belt, but it is helpful to read ahead.
Part 3: Appendix and References – Summaries and other useful info.

Introduction

The Korean Academy of Taekwondo (KAT) is one of Colorado's oldest and most successful martial arts schools. Since we were founded in 1980, we have produced numerous state, local, and international champions and have been a positive force in the community.

The core philosophy of the school is to provide a blend of traditional and modern training. Traditional training has long been valued for its emphasis on discipline, order, and self-sacrifice. Modern training has been valued for its emphasis on creativity, utility, and openness. We try to blend the two by training with modern techniques using a traditional mindset. Except for certain requirements, techniques are not adhered to simply because "that's the way it's always been done," but rather because that is the way that the technique works best. There are small changes in our curriculum as better ways of training and competing evolve.

Besides Traditional and Olympic Taekwondo, we also train in other martial arts techniques in order to complement our style and provide the necessary skills for defense of self and others.

About This Book

This handbook is the official textbook for students in all the KAT Network programs. It contains sections written by numerous masters and advanced black belt students who have been very successful both in competing and teaching what they know to others. The handbook was compiled and edited by Master Bill Pottle and Master Katie Pottle, and unless otherwise indicated, they are responsible for developing the content of each section or addressing the students using the first person.

Korean words are usually italicized throughout the text. As always check with *Sabumnim* for the most detailed requirements and proper technical guidance. This book cannot replace qualified martial arts instruction, and it has no intention to do so. It is merely a supplemental learning aide to help make our students improve more efficiently.

This book is about how to do martial arts, but as your martial arts journey progresses you may find great value in the companion books, *Teaching Martial Arts: A Practical Guide* and *The Way of the Dojo: Owning and Operating Your Own Martial Arts School.* These two books cover topics associated with how to teach martial arts and also how to successfully run a martial arts school.

Young children may also enjoy *The Princess and the Ogre: Martial Arts Fairy Tales and Nursery Rhymes.* You can see all our current martial arts books at www.billpottle.com/martial-arts/

At the Beginning

Complete this phase when you first begin training or receive this handbook, regardless of your belt level.

Name: Date:

Why did I begin Taekwondo training?

What are my goals for my training? What do I expect to get out of it?

Who are my closest friends that I can train with?

Explain the meaning of Taekwondo.

Online Resources

KAT takes full advantage of technological innovations in order to provide clear and rapid communication between all KAT members.

Web Pages

The school web page is a great resource for the most up to date information as well as multimedia files and tournament registration. The web page has blogs, Google Calendar, videos of requirements, history, and much more. The web page can be found at:

www.kattaekwondo.com

Facebook- Click 'like' and 'Get Notifications' on our Facebook page. You'll receive updates and be able to see pictures and videos posted to the site by students and instructors. Remember, Facebook will probably **NOT** show you content posted here, so it's good to visit regularly.

www.facebook.com/kattkd

Youtube - KAT maintains a robust Youtube channel that features videos of all of the requirements, as well as highlight videos from various tournaments and events.

www.youtube.com/kattkd

Wikidrills - KAT developed this website to be similar to wikipedia, but for martial arts training drills and martial arts techniques. You can see how different techniques go together (i.e., what counters what) or how to train certain attributes.

www.wikidrills.com

Colorado Martial Arts News – More in-depth reporting about various event results, interviews with key figures, product reviews, etc.

www.coloradomanews.com

USA Poomsae Team – The US National Poomsae team has an extremely helpful site that features videos of our top athletes performing their forms at international championships as well as an athlete reference guide that is a must read.

www.poomsae-usa.com

Kukkiwon – This important site has much valuable information, including terminology and technical info at the World Taekwondo Academy

www.kukkiwon.or.kr/

Kukkiwon Management System – The KMS is responsible for the database of Dan holders around the world. You can check anyone's status and 4th Dan and above can submit applications for their students.

kms.kukkiwon.or.kr/

Levels of Self-Defense

A true martial artist does not need to prove himself to people on the street. Instead, come to the dojang and prove yourself against people who know what they are doing. You must only progress to a higher level of self-defense once a previous level has failed to resolve the conflict.

First Level - Avoid The Situation - The first level of self-defense is to avoid situations that may put you at risk. In fact, the vast majority of confrontations can be avoided by simply walking away.

Second Level - Verbal Defense - The second level of self-defense is to use words to avoid fighting. Use humor, offer the aggressor an exit where he does not lose face, or simply refuse to fight. Remain calm and in control and do not show fear.

Third Level – Restrain or Disable Opponent - The third level of self-defense is to use grappling techniques to restrain and disable your opponent. You may hold them in a dominant position or apply locks and chokes that can stop your opponent without causing them any permanent damage. If you are in school it is best to hold them in a dominant position until a teacher comes.

Forth Level – Strike Opponent - The forth level of self-defense is to use striking techniques to attack the opponent. Striking techniques often cause injury to the opponent and can cause you to mix body fluids with your opponent. These techniques should only be used as a last resort

Chapter 1: Fundamental Problem of Martial Arts

All martial arts start with this problem, and the way that they answer it is perhaps the most important factor that drives their development. To put it in one sentence:

- **How can you become good at hurting people without hurting people?**

  Or

- **How do you practice dangerous things safely?**

Thus, instructors are always trying to make things as real as possible without subjecting their students to undue risk. Different martial arts have different ways around it. In some forms of Karate, they have all sparring be light contact only, and stop after a point may have been scored. In Olympic Style Taekwondo, we wear pads, and limit techniques and targets, while allowing full force. In One Step Sparring, we use moves like elbow to the spine, but do so with no contact. In grappling, there is some time between pain is felt and when injury occurs. By signaling to the partner during this time to stop, students can train full out while avoiding injury. This tap out is a key component of grappling.

Perhaps advanced Virtual Reality and Augmented Reality technologies in the future will allow training that at least seems fully realistic while also being safe. If so this will be a key advance in the history of martial arts.

In KAT, we will train many different ways, thus gaining the benefits of each. Let's take a minute to see these ways in more detail.

Why Grapple?

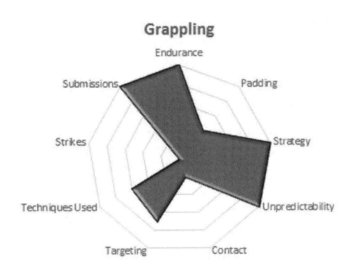

Grappling

Endurance · Padding · Strategy · Unpredictability · Contact · Targeting · Techniques Used · Strikes · Submissions

Grappling is an extremely important part of our training. Prior to the 1990s, there was some gulf between striking arts and grappling arts. Striking arts like Taekwondo, Kung Fu, and Karate had a doctrine of *'one hit, one kill.'* This meant that they would develop strikes so powerful and accurate that they would be able to end the fight quickly. They reasoned that their powerful strikes would overwhelm any attacker before the attacker could take them to the ground.

There was one critical flaw in this way of thinking, however— it simply wasn't true. The late 1990s saw a dramatic shift in martial arts techniques with the advent of **Mixed Martial Arts (MMA)** competitions such as the Ultimate Fighting Championship, PRIDE, and K1. With few exceptions, grapplers won time after time. An obscure Brazilian family, the Gracies, was catapulted into the spotlight. Forward-thinking masters around the world began to take notice.

At the KAT, the heart has always been Taekwondo. However, Sport Taekwondo and actual fighting are two very different endeavors. We train in grappling enough so that if confronted on the street with an attacker who is a superior striker, we will be able to take them down and choke them out. If we meet an attacker who is a superior grappler, we will be able to avoid being choked or submitted enough to use our striking power.

Taekwondo sparring guides us well until the clinch position. In a match, the referee breaks both competitors after the clinch. Thus, for the purposes of our practical self-defense, most of it *begins* in the clinch, and goes to submission. Thus we cover a critical hole in our technique that most Taekwondo schools do not address.

Another important reason to do grappling is that in many ways, it is the inverse of Olympic style sparring. For instance, things that are legal in grappling, i.e., chokes, takedowns, grabs, locks, throws, are illegal in sparring. Conversely, things that are legal in sparring like kicks and punches are illegal in grappling. Thus, this is one way that we can get around the fundamental problem of martial arts.

Why Forms?

Forms, or memorized patterns of movement, first originated as a way for students to practice their techniques without direct supervision by their master instructor. Now, forms are one of the

most traditional parts of Taekwondo. They allow students to practice their hand techniques, stances, and kicks and learn how to move. The stances and techniques that are practiced in forms are generally not the same as those used in sparring. Forms should be performed with synchronized timing. Seeing an entire class moving with precision and confidence at the exact same time is a very beautiful thing. Plus, there is a great benefit of striving towards a perfect technical standard.

Why One Steps?

One steps are very important to our curriculum for several reasons, but they are **not** 'plug and play.' You will never use the one steps exactly as taught in real self-defense, because no one will attack you with long stance punch as we do in one steps. However, you will learn timing, distance, vital striking points, and how to combine strikes, throws and takedowns into fluid motions. One steps also provide an outlet for creativity in the higher belts.

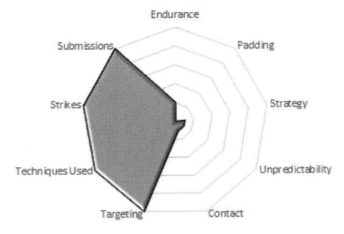

Why Olympic Sparring?

Sparring is important in that it provides a 'reality check' on your training. It also helps you know how to be hit, how to read an opponent, how to perform under pressure, etc. The sport aspect of it can motivate training and it's a common language with which we can interface with other schools.

Why Terminology?

It is important to study Korean terminology for several reasons. First of all, it is a part of our shared culture and heritage and martial artists. Korean words can also serve as a bridge between other cultures. We have had many established black belts from other countries join KAT and then we can all call techniques by the same name.

There are several important things to remember. First, due to the Romanization of Korean words, sometimes the same word will have several different spellings when using English letters. Secondly, many newer techniques are referred to in English because they were made by non-Korean speakers or come from other martial arts. For instance, although there are certainly Korean words for things like Cover Punch, Electronic *Hogu*, Butterfly Twist, Ariel, Fast Kick or Webster, few outside of Korea use them.

Overall

Now that you see *why* the different curriculum components are important and *how* they fit together, you can understand 'the big idea' on how KAT curriculum is structured

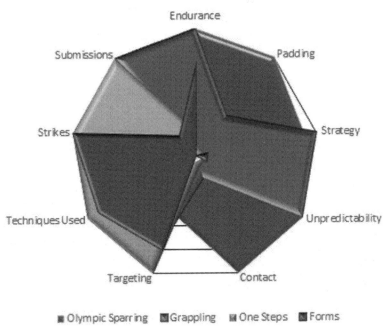

KAT Curriculum Components

■ Olympic Sparring ■ Grappling ■ One Steps ■ Forms

Chapter 2: Stances

Having a proper stance is very important to traditional techniques. In general, when knees are to be bent, they should be bent so that you just can't see your feet when looking down.

Attention Stance
(*Moa Sugi*)

Feet are together and closed, and both knees are bent. This is the stance for the *charyut* command. Both feet face forwards.

Relaxed Stance

(*Naranhi Sugi*)

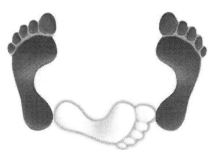

Feet are one foot length apart. Both legs are straight. This is the stance for *junbi* and listening stance. Both feet face straight forwards.

Walking Stance
(*Ap Sugi*)

Walking stance is also known as short stance or short forward stance. The insides of the feet are on the opposite sides of the same line and one foot apart. The back foot can be slightly rotated to the outside, up to 30 degrees.

Long Stance
(*Ap Kubi*)

Long stance (in 3rd edition called Mid Stance) is used in WTF Forms. The back foot is rotated 30 degrees, and the front knee is bent so that you don't see your toes.

There is one fist distance between the inside edges of your feet.

One Fist

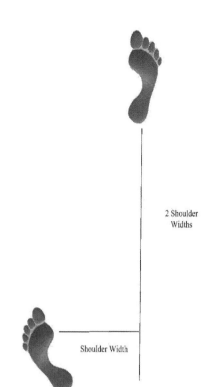

Traditional Long Stance (*Ap Kubi*)

Long stance is a traditional stance not used in WTF forms. The feet are shoulder width apart and the front foot is two shoulder widths in front of the back one.

The front knee is bent so that you don't see you toes.

Long stance is also used for holding boards or other targets.

Horse Stance (*Juchoom Sugi*)

In horse stance you must bend both knees so that you don't see your toes. There is also **Extended Horse Stance** for ITF forms and other traditional practices. In Extended Horse Stance your feet are two shoulder width distances apart.

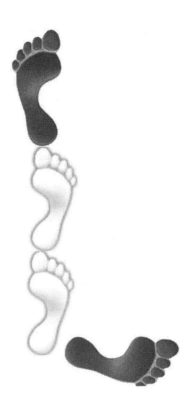

Back Stance
(Dwit Kubi)

In back stance you bend both of your knees, placing most of the weight on the back one. The inside edge of your feet line up, which is slightly different than the traditional back stance when the heels are on the same line. Back foot is turned 90 degrees to the side. Chest can also be turned slightly to the side. Don't lean too far back or forwards.

Left/Right Stance
(Wen/Oren Sugi)

Each stance occurs only once, in the first line of *Tae Guek* 5. Both knees are straight and the weight is evenly distributed on each foot.

Tiger Stance
(Bum Sugi)

In tiger stance you place one foot in front of the other with the insides of the feet on the same lines. The front foot is up and both knees are bent. Almost all of the weight is on the back leg. Back foot may again be rotated out slightly, up to 30 degrees.

A variation of this is **Assisted Stance** (*kyotdari sugi*) where the back foot is the one up and the ball of the rear foot is aligned with the arch of the front foot. This stance is not used until the 8th *Dan* form.

Another variation of this is **Kendo Stance**, where the front foot is on the ground and back is up, and the feet are shoulder distance apart. This stance is used with weapons.

Crane Stance (*Hakdari Sugi*)

Crane stance is where one foot is on the ground and the other foot rests in the knee. It can be both Forward Crane Stance (as in Demo 6) or Side Crane Stance (as in *Keumgang*). In Side Crane Stance, the other knee should be bent and to the side of the standing leg. The height should be the same as Horse Stance. Although it is used only in the black belt forms, it can be an excellent way to practice balance.

Crossed Stance (*Koa Sugi*)

Crossed stance is where you cross one foot behind the other. It comes as both Back Crossed Stance (as in OSS#3, TG5) or Front Crossed Stance (as in *Chil Jang*). There is one fist width between the feet and the front leg bears most of the weight. Both knees bend.

Sparring Stance

The sparring stance is not fixed, it will change with each student and with different circumstances. However, the 'textbook' stance involves the chest being turned to the side and the feet turned about thirty degrees. The heals are on the same line or close to it and both knees are bent. Whole feet are shown, but you generally are bouncing on the balls of your feet.

Fighting Stance

In real self defense situations, we turn the chest more to the front and the feet turn more to the front. Again, this varies with personal preference. Turning to the front opens us more to frontal attack but also allows for back hand strikes, and applying and defending double leg takedowns. Hands must be up to defend the head.

Striking Surfaces

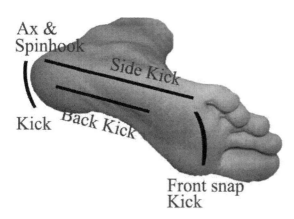

Ax &
Spinhook

Side Kick

Kick Back Kick

Front snap
Kick

Out to In Crescent Kick

Roundhouse Kick

In to Out Crescent Kick

Taekwondo is known for the number, speed, and power of our kicking techniques. Here are the main kicks and notes on executing them.

The pictures to the left show the different striking surfaces of the foot and which kicks they are used for. Note that no kicks are done with the toes. It is important to strike with the correct part of the foot to get maximum power. Some kicks may use different parts of the foot, for instance, ax kick and spin hook kick may be done with the ball of the foot for greater range.

Main Kicks

Front Kick (*Ap Chaggie*) - In this kick, you bring your knee up to your chest and snap it out, kicking with the ball of your foot. Then, you return your foot to the normal position.

Roundhouse Kick (*Tylo Chaggie*) - The many variations of this kick are the most used techniques in Taekwondo. You bring your leg straight from the ground, and then turn your hips to bring it into your target. The power comes mostly from the hip. Developing an effective roundhouse kick should be a top priority for any competitor. There are five types of roundhouse kicks:

- **Back Leg Roundhouse** – Also called just roundhouse, turn your hips and kick with the back leg.

- **Receiving Kick** (*Pada Chaggie*) – This is called a receiving kick because you receive your partner's attack and counterattack at the same time. It is done with the back leg but both legs move together. It can be done in the same place or while fading backwards.

- **Butterfly Kick** ("360 Roundhouse" *narabam*) -This kick is a 360 degree roundhouse with the front foot. It is useful to build up momentum and cover distance. It is important to make a tight spin, thus you will increase angular momentum and deliver a more powerful kick.

- *Ap Bahl* – This is a kick with the front foot where you pick up your foot without moving your planted foot. It is the least powerful of all roundhouse kicks, but can still be powerful enough to score. Works well as part of a double or to the head.

- **Fast Kick** – Here you slide forward and deliver your roundhouse. It is useful for covering distance, scoring points, of feeling out an opponent.

Double Kicks - By doubles it is meant multiple roundhouse kicks. Doubles can be made from any of the 5 types of roundhouse kicks. These are extremely useful kicks. These kicks can hit an opponent on both the closed and open side, and are also are very effective at blocking counter attacks.

Side Kick (*Yup Chaggie*) - The body is turned 180 degrees and the foot is brought to the chest and then released. In order to perform this kick correctly, you must hit the target with the heel and edge of your foot. Your whole body should be aligned.

Ax Kick (*Chicki Chagggie*) - This kick is often used for board breaking because of its power. The foot is brought straight up above the head, and then smashing down on the target. A slightly modified form is useful in sparring as well. When attacking with the front leg, bend your knee to pass over your opponent's shoulder.

Crescent Kicks (*Bahndall Chaggie*) - There are both Outside to Inside crescent kicks (Outside) and Inside to Outside crescent kicks (Inside). You sweep your foot up in a crescent motion to hit the opponent on the side of the head. Use the side of your foot.

Back kick (*Dwi Chaggie*) - This kick is accomplished by turning your body 90 degrees and then by kicking straight backwards, making contact with the heel of your foot. It is a very useful counter attack. In the *National Geographic Fight Science* show, a step in back kick generated over 1700 lbs of force.

Hook Kick - You bring your foot up like a sidekick but instead hook over to hit the side of the headgear.

Spin Hook Kick ("Reverse Turning Kick" "Spin Whip Kick" "Spin Wheel Kick") - This kick is much like back kick, except instead of going straight back, the foot hooks over to make contact with the side of the headgear. While this technique can be accomplished in a fraction of a second, it is still considerably slower than most techniques and leaves the kicker open for a counter attack, and therefore is used only infrequently. However, it is extremely powerful, and accounts for the majority of knockouts in the adult black belt divisions. (Out of concern for safety, knockouts and hard head contact are usually not permitted in other divisions.)

Push Kick ("Cut Kick") -This kick is used as a setup for other kicks, usually not to score by itself. You bring your foot up to your chest, and then place it on your opponent's chest protector and push off. It is useful for disrupting the opponent's rhythm. It can also be used to cut their momentum when they are charging in. It is being used to score more recently with the advent of electronic *hogus*.

Infrequently Used Kicks

Sometimes, kicks that are 'unorthodox' can be effectively used to disrupt an opponent or make them hesitate for a split second.

Twist Kick- This is like a roundhouse kick, but instead you twist your foot inside and kick with your knee rotated laterally. This kick used to work well... until they invented chest protectors. I have only infrequently observed a serious competitor using it on purpose.

Pancake Kick – This kick comes up like a roundhouse kick, but if the opponent tries to jam you, you flip your hips over and kick with the top of your foot pointing downwards.

Advanced Kicks

All kicks can be modified or done immediately following a spin to increase power. Spins of more than 360 degrees are generally used only for demonstration purposes instead of during sparring. Thus there can be 360 side kick or 360 crescent kick as well.

360 Ax Kick- This is like a butterfly kick, but instead of hitting with a roundhouse you hit with an ax kick or outside crescent kick.

360 Degree Back Kick -In this kick, you do a back kick, but spin to your inside to deliver it. You can also add in a cut kick first to hit the opponent twice.

360 Degree Hook Kick – Same as back kick but finishes with hook.

Demo Kicks

540 – This kick doesn't really involve 540 degrees, but we've adopted the convention used by other schools. It's a butterfly kick where you land on the kicking leg.

Swipe – Horizontal 540 kick that hits a target above you.

540 Hook Kick – This kick starts out with the 540 above, but you spin around and throw a hook kick with the leg that did not do the butterfly kick.

720 Roundhouse – Spin twice in the air and then kick.

L Kick ("Nike Kick") – This kick comes from Capoeira. You land on one arm and kick up with your other leg.

Kung Fu Butterfly Kick – Jump off one leg, let your body hang in the air horizontally, and land on the other leg.

Butterfly Twist – This kick is like a horizontal 360 degree spin and is very difficult.

There are many other kicks and kicking combinations possible. In fact, new kicks and modifications of existing kicks are being made all the time. However, the preceding kicks are all the major ones that any Taekwondoist needs to know.

Chapter 4: Hand Techniques

Striking Surfaces

It is critical to use the proper striking surface when using your hands to strike or block.

Note that in Taekwondo the wrist is almost never bent.

See the following three diagrams for the Ridge Hand, Knife Hand, Spear Fingers, Punch, Hammer Fist, and Back Fist striking surfaces. They are customarily written as one word (i.e, knifehand.)

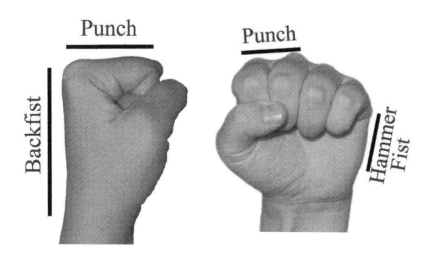

Blocks

The following table illustrates many of the basic blocking moves and their chamber and ending positions. Remember that the blocking hand generally chambers on **the outside.**

Move	Starting (Chamber) Position	Ending Position
Low Block	Blocking hand towards face at shoulder level. Other arm is straight and facing towards blocking leg.	In front of thigh and two fist widths above
Middle Block	On opposite hip.	Even with shoulder line. Not in WTF forms.
Sweeping Middle Block	Arm bent at 90o and facing backwards	Across center line. Fist even with shoulder.
Turning Middle Block	Same as middle block.	Turn fist outside.
High Block	Palm facing inside, in front of hip.	Wrist at centerline of face, one fist in front and one fist above forehead. Elbow ends bent at ~110°
Low Guarding Block	Chamber hand palm down, blocking hand palm up and angled 30o upwards	Same as low block and other hand is on sternum one palm distance away.
Middle Guarding Block	Chamber straight out on opposite side of body, blocking hand facing inwards, striking hand facing down.	Front hand facing palm away from body back hand facing up and in front of sternum.
High Guarding Block	Same as Middle Guarding Block	Front hand same as Middle Guarding Block, back hand same as high block

The following table summarizes more advanced hand techniques and their chambering and ending positions.

Advanced Block	Starting (Chamber) Position	Ending Position Notes
Low X Block	Palms facing up near armpits	Crossed in front of waist. Front hand on the outside.
Middle X Block	Same as Low	Crossed in front of sternum
High X Block	Palms facing up on waist	Crossed one fist above and in front of forehead
Push Block	Arm bent at 90o and hand open. Twist body away from blocking point.	Across centerline
Pole Block	Same as Middle Knifehand Guarding Block	Thumbs out, top hand facing down, bottom hand facing up. Lean in
Diamond Block	Like Low Block and High Block	High block hand on outside
Scissors Block	Chamber in final position on opposite side.	Low block and middle block to the front Middle block hand goes on outside.
Double Middle Forearm Block	Cross low with palms facing down.	Both hands do Middle Block to the front. Hands are even with shoulders.
Double High Forearm Block	Cross in front of face with palms facing in	Like turning middle block but hands slightly more than shoulder distance wide.
Mountain Block		Both hands out in middle block position and forearms parallel to ground

The following knifehand blocks are done analogous to the blocks in parenthesis: **Knifehand Low Block** (Low Block), **Knifehand Middle Block** (Turning Middle Block), **Knifehand High Block** (High Block), and **Knifehand Low, Middle, and High Guarding blocks** (Low, Middle, and High Guarding Blocks).

All knifehands chamber with knifehands. If not specified, the technique should be done with a closed fist.

While all blocking techniques chamber on the outside, striking techniques chamber on the inside, and proceed straight to the target. Blocking techniques are meant to sweep through an area to be of maximum effect.

Strikes

The following table lists the main strikes in Taekwondo. Note there are other blocks and strikes, as well as exceptions to the chambering rules. These cases are few and treated individually by instructors.

Strike	Starting (Chamber) Position	Ending Position
Punch	Fist palm up on hip.	Even with sternum
High Punch	Fist palm up on hip	Halfway between nose and mouth
Knifehand	Same as low block but open	Even with target
Ridgehand	Same as punch	Even with target
Spearfingers	Open hand palm up on ribs	Sternum or other soft target
Front Backfist	Fist in armpit of other arm, palm down	Halfway between nose and mouth. Arm bent at 100o
Side Backfist	Fist in armpit of other arm, palm down	Even with target. Arm slightly bent
Hammerfist	Fist in armpit of other shoulder.	Top of head
Tiger's Mouth	Fist palm up on hips. Open	Even with throat. Palm flat.
Palm Strike	Fist palm up on hip and open	Even with target
Turning Palm Strike	Same as palm strike	To jaw
Elbow Strike	Fist palm up on hip meets palm of support hand	Attack jaw and palm of closed fist faces down,
Elbow Smash	Non-striking hand opens and reaches out. Striking hand comes from normal chamber position	End at solar plexus with forearm parallel to ground.

Part 2: Belt Curriculum

Official Belt Ranks:

White Belt – 10th *Gup*
Yellow Belt – 9th *Gup*
High Yellow Belt – 8th *Gup*
Green Belt – 7th *Gup*
High Green Belt – 6th *Gup*
Blue Belt – 5th *Gup*
High Blue Belt – 4th *Gup*
Red Belt – 3rd *Gup*
High Red Belt – 2nd *Gup*
Double Black Stripe Red Belt – 1st *Gup*
1st *Dan* Black Belt
2nd *Dan* Black Belt
3rd *Dan* Black Belt
4th *Dan* Black Belt – Master
5th *Dan* Black Belt – Master
6th *Dan* Black Belt – Master
7th *Dan* Black Belt – Master
8th *Dan* Black Belt – Grand Master
9th *Dan* Black Belt – Grand Master
10th *Dan* Black Belt (*Honorary*) – Grand Master

Curriculum Paths/Modifications

The vast majority of students will continue through the regular curriculum, which has been thoughtfully designed and has consistently produced high quality black belts for decades. However, we have students of all ages from two to senior citizens and all levels from special needs to Olympic athletes. Therefore we have also implemented the following curriculum modifications.

Tiger Cubs (2-3 Year Olds)

Tiger Cubs has 5 modules (Balance, Coordination, Focus, Confidence, and Safety). Each module lasts 2 months and students receive t-shirts based on the number of modules they have completed. Parents do the class with their children.

Little Tigers (3-4 Year Olds)

The Little Tigers class gives students a head start on the regular program. Students earn white belts with yellow, green, blue, and red stripes for completing part of the regular white belt curriculum. So, the curriculum is the same, but it's broken down into more manageable chunks. See the full Little Tigers requirements in the back.

Silver Tigers (35+ Year Olds)

The Silver Tigers curriculum is mostly the same as the main one, but it is more self-defence based and less sports based. Most of the ground grappling is replaced with standing grappling. There is also much less contact sparring. For black belt degrees of 2nd and up, students must also complete their choice of various Accomplishments and Performances.

Advanced Black Belts (Competitors)

All KAT black belts go through the regular curriculum on their first black belt test, but high level competitors are allowed to go through a modified version for 2nd *Dan* testing and above. In order to be eligible for either the forms or sparring track, you must have won a medal in the black belt division of the US National Championships or any major international tournament.

KAT Tactics

The KAT Tactics program is a rigorous and advanced program that covers important topics in the realm of self-defense that are not traditionally considered part of most martial arts. This class is organized into rotating modules that are offered periodically and the training is open to adults as well as certain KAT black belts.

Sample modules include **InfoSEC** (Encryption, Securing home networks, using computers without leaving traces, etc), **WildSEC** (Advanced wilderness survival skills, tracking, signaling, etc), **MedSEC** (Beyond basic first aid when medical help is unavailable, etc), **Gun and Knife Training**, etc. See Master Bill for more information.

White Belt 10th *Gup*

Congratulations on taking the first step to becoming happier, healthier, and safer! With each belt you earn, study the relevant section of the handbook and answer all of the questions in the back section before the promotion test.

White Belt Key Points

- Learn the basics of how to be a student – What we are studying and why, how to participate in class, etc.

- Start to develop good habits in both your techniques and how you practice.

- Learn about all the different resources that KAT has created to help you.

Lesson: Basics and Philosophy

Three Components of Practice

Taekwondo has come to mean many different things over time, and in the end each school owner is responsible for setting the direction that his or her school will take. At KAT we focus on three distinct components of training. Each has its own separate rules, techniques, and mindset.

The first component is the **Traditional Taekwondo** component. Here we practice the forms, one step sparring and other techniques that are practiced all over the world and have been practiced and passed down through the generations. The emphasis here is on power, accuracy, and technical proficiency. There is not much evolution of technique in this component.

The second component is the **Sport Taekwondo** component. Here we compete in the Olympic sport of Taekwondo. We follow the competition rules that limit available techniques. Because competition is done in a public venue, techniques evolve rapidly as people see what works and what doesn't. The emphasis is on speed and utility. Most recently Sport Poomsae has taken hold in the sport aspect of Taekwondo, allowing for high level competition in forms alongside sparring.

The third component is the **Practical Self Defense** component. Here we practice our grappling and other associated techniques. There are no 'rules' in the street situation (although of course laws will still apply) and the supreme ideal of this component is utility—whether or not a given technique works in a given situation. Thus techniques evolve fairly rapidly in this component as well.

Philosophy of Taekwondo

Taekwondo is much more than just a physical activity. The teaching of the art of Taekwondo has long carried with it an entire culture and philosophy, and this will guide your interactions with others both within and outside of Taekwondo practice. The Taekwondo philosophy is rooted in the common spirit of martial arts practice and the culture of the Korean people, which both draw heavily on Confucian and Taoist ideas.

'*Tae*' literally means to kick or strike with the foot, '*Kwon*' means to punch or strike with the hand, and '*Do*' means the way. Thus, Taekwondo could be translated as "The Way of Kicking and Punching." Of the three components, *Do* is by far the most important. As you age your physical technique will fade, but if trained well, your *Do* will always burn strongly.

The Taekwondo school is like a large extended family. Everyone looks out for everyone else, with senior students exercising the most responsibility. We don't judge others, but accept them and help them progress and grow not only in the martial arts, but at school, work, and in the community.

In addition, Taekwondo has evolved other guiding principles that come directly from the study of sparring situations. For example, one should do something fully or not at all. Attacking halfway can be dangerous— it is better to attack full out or not attack at all. Taekwondo techniques are also focused primarily on what works in a competition situation. You must find a way to win based on your attributes and who you are competing with. Hard and honest work is highly appreciated. No one will be watching you to make sure you touch your chin on every push up, but not doing so only hurts yourself and your team. Also, if you have a condition or injury that prevents you from doing a particular drill, do something else that you can do instead. If you are too injured or sick, then **do not** work out. Working out too much while sick or injured can cause you to miss more classes, and can possibly get your teammates sick as well. You should still come to class and help hold pads for your teammates. You must be able to bounce back from both your wins as well as your losses.

Perhaps above all consistency is valued. Consistent attendance is something everyone can achieve, regardless of their skill level or athletic talent.

How to Tie a Belt

There is a proper way to tie a Taekwondo belt. Although there are several different methods, they all end up with the same result. The following is an easy to understand method.
First, find the middle of the belt by lining up the ends. There should be no twists in your belt. Place the middle of the belt over your belly button.

Next, wrap the belt around the back. When the two ends meet, one end must go under and one must stay over. This is critical to ensure that your belt does not cross in the back. The forth picture shows what it will look like in the front.

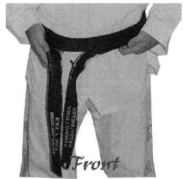

Wrap the side that was over under **both** strands of the belt. To finish the knot, keep the upper strand on top, and then tie it through the strand that was on the bottom as shown. In the picture, the strand pointing down will come up and to the person's right. It is also called a square knot.

There are three key aspects of a correctly tied belt. First, the **ends are even**. Second, the knot is the **correct 'fortune cookie' knot**, with both ends facing out sideways. Third, the belt is **not crossed in the back**.

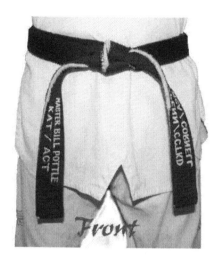

Etiquette

Taekwondo etiquette is very important in your development. It demonstrates discipline and respect to fellow members in the school and to other martial artists. Taekwondo has evolved from Confucian ideals of respect and harmony in relationships between two people. In general, always show a high degree of respect for all your fellow martial artists.

Posture– Make sure that when bowing, you begin from an 'attention' position. There are two proper ways to sit. One is with the legs crossed and hands on the knees, (Sitting Position 1) and the other is with your knees bent and your legs folded underneath you (Sitting Position 2).

(Sitting Position 1)   (Sitting Position 2)

Entering/Exiting the dojang- When entering and exiting the matted area, you must bow once to the flags. This is a sign of respect for our country and training area. It is very important to do this when visiting other dojangs as well.

Addressing- Always use "sir" for males and "ma'am" for females when speaking to any instructor, regardless of their age. Use the same for adults regardless of their rank.

Uniform- Proper care and maintenance of your uniform is very important. It must be kept clean and folded neatly. Always wear your uniform appropriately with your belt tied tightly across the waist. Do not eat in your uniform.

Do not wash your belt. Your belt represents all the hard work you have accomplished in Taekwondo, and washing it is symbolically like washing out your training. Only adjust your uniform during breaks when you have stopped and finished a drill. In doing so, you must turn away from the flags and higher ranks. If you do not have or happen to forget your uniform, you should at least wear *dobok* pants and a t-shirt for class. Wear only a plain white shirt or an official KAT shirt. There are will be some informal workouts where you do not need your uniform (i.e., grappling class). If you forget your belt, stand in the rear of the class behind those who are properly dressed. Do 30 pushups

Knowledge- Only learn the forms and one step sparring techniques up to and including your rank. To learn anything higher than your current level is showing disrespect for the ranking system and higher ranks. All ranks should try to learn all of the grappling drills if possible. Black belts may learn all forms.

Testing

The belt tests are a time for students who are ready to advance in rank to show their progress to the school and community. The test is less of a time to evaluate whether or not you have learned your material than it is a time for you to show what you have learned and to show a positive attitude. In order to be eligible to test, students must have good attendance and earn the **testing application** by showing some of your requirements in front of the class. Tests are the most formal occasions that we have in our school, so all of the rules of etiquette are extra important.

When you turn in your application, you must also turn in your report card (or a note from your parents) and this book. If you are under 18, your parents must also fill out a report of how you are doing at home on the back. **Students must have good grades to promote to the next belt level.** Also, a student who gets straight As in school (or equivalent) and also on each part of the promotion test will be eligible to skip to the next rank. Skip ranks are very rare, but can be used to reward exceptional students.

If you do well on the test but have problems with one or two parts, you will be required to retest only on the parts you failed. Retests can be done in the days after the test and before the belt ceremony.

The belt ceremony is usually a few days after the test for the main school and the Wednesday after the test at Metro. In the main school we brew a special belt ceremony tea that is made only for belt ceremonies. There are fourteen secret ingredients, one of which you will learn with every belt you earn. Be sure to take lots of pictures with your group at each new rank— these pictures will be very valuable when you are all testing for black belt.

Dojang Rules

The dojang rules have been developed for two main purposes. The first is **safety**. We are practicing a martial art, and it is impossible to avoid all injuries. However, by keeping safety foremost in mind, we can avoid most of them. The second purpose is **efficiency**. We come here to learn, and the more efficiently we do it, the better our entire class becomes. It is not fair for one person to disrupt the class for the others.

1. Show respect to all of your fellow students, especially your higher ranks and those older than you. Address all adults as "Sir" or "Ma'm"
2. Only TKD shoes and bare feet are allowed in the training area.
3. Bow to the flags when entering and leaving the dojang.
4. No free sparring or grappling without Sabumnim's approval.
5. No chewing gum, alcohol or smoking inside the dojang.
6. Keep your uniform, body, and language clean. Keep your dojang clean.
7. Remove watches and jewelry before training.
8. Show up for class on time and ready to work out both mentally and physically.
9. No unnecessary talking or laughing during class.
10. Face away from the flag and your seniors while adjusting your uniform
11. Do not leave class without permission.

Lesson: Board Breaking Basics

Board (or brick) breaking is an important part of our examinations and demonstrations. Breaking allows us to practice the full power of our techniques on an inanimate object. Breaking provides an important reality check because the board either breaks or it doesn't. It also allows students to overcome their fears and gain real confidence in their techniques. It helps students to see through physical limitations. In upper levels, breaking is used to demonstrate difficult techniques.

Breaking Tips

The mechanics of board breaking are interesting and helpful to study. In order to break a board, one must cause a shearing moment in the board that is larger than the critical moment for that particular piece of wood. This is determined by various factors in the wood, such as the dimensions, material, imperfections, etc. Certain factors matter more than others, doubling the thickness of a board can increase the difficulty more than doubling the length.

Now, the shearing moment that you must overcome is a product of the force you are able to transmit and the perpendicular distance between the points where the board is being held. This is why it is very difficult to break the 'short boards' that have already been broken once. Also, if the holders hold the board closer to the edges, it will be easier for you to break.

The amount of force you can deliver is fixed by the strength of your muscles, but when you strike a target, you deliver an impulse to it. An impulse is the product of a force and a time. Therefore, the shorter you are in contact with the board, the larger the force component of the impulse will be, and the easier it will break.

However, the holders are every bit as important to the successful break as the breaker. When holders can hold on both sides of the board, the board is in double shear. When they hold it only on one end, the board is in single shear only, and is twice as difficult to break. However, unless the board is fastened to something secure like a wall, part of your energy will go into delivering a bending moment to the board as well that will cause it to rotate about the axis that it is being held by. This will make it more than twice as difficult to break when the board is only held in one spot.

This is also why some holders will back up other holders in an attempt to keep the board perfectly steady. If the holders allow the board to come back, it will soften your blow on it. This phenomenon is useful to soften a blow during sparring, as you draw part of your body back.

True free breaks, with no support at all, are incredibly difficult, since there is no supporting force. They must be done with a large amount of speed.

Things to keep in mind:
Dry boards will be more brittle and break easier than wet ones.

If the board does not move, the impulse will be transferred back to you as well. Therefore, the faster you hit, the shorter time the force is transferred. Also, if the board does not break, it may hurt because a large force is transferred back to your body for a relatively long time.

Spacers between multiple boards will make it easier to penetrate because each board is considered separately, and not as a whole block of wood.

Before a powerful kick is attempted, make sure that a flying board will not damage anyone or anything. This is especially important with breaks that are only held in one spot.

Boards must always be broken with the grain. Although they can be broken against it, the forces necessary are large.

How to Break a Board

After considering all of the above, you should first chose a technique that you are comfortable with.

1. Set up the board and holders

2. Practice the technique slowly about three times while breathing and gathering your internal energy.

3. Yell loudly.

4. Yell again as you attack the board with all of your force. Remember, the harder you hit it the less it will hurt.

5. Bow to the judges or audience and collect your pieces

Testing Requirements

Chun Ji- 19 Movements

Chun Ji is a lake at the top of a mountain just on the North Korean side of their border with China. It means *"Heaven and Earth"* or *"Where Land Meets Sky."* The pattern makes two crosses, one representing the land and one the sky.

Chun Ji has 19 counts but only three different moves. You 'follow your hand' or turn 90 degrees to the left whenever your left hand is out and 180 degrees to the right whenever your right hand is out. The following diagram can help you to understand which way to go. Each direction change represents two moves (a block and punch).

```
                  [8]
                  [3]
 [6][1]                        [2][5]
                  [4]
                  [7]
```

Assuming your start facing the north, the 19 movements are

1. Long Stance and Low Block (W)
2. Long Stance and Punch (W)
3. Long Stance and Low Block (E)
4. Long Stance and Punch (E)
5. Long Stance and Low Block (N)
6. Long Stance and Punch (N)
7. Long Stance and Low Block (S)
8. Long Stance and Punch (S)
9. Back Stance and Middle Block (E)
10. Long Stance and Punch (E)
11. Back Stance and Middle Block (W)
12. Long Stance and Punch (W)
13. Back Stance and Middle Block (S)
14. Long Stance and Punch (S)
15. Back Stance and Middle Block (N)
16. Long Stance and Punch (N)
17. Long Stance and Punch (N)
18. Step Back, Long Stance and Punch (N)
19. Step Back, Long Stance and Punch (N) – (*kihap*)

Chun Ji Cheat Sheet

Chun Ji Key Points

- Make sure your different stances look different! Long Stance has the back leg straight while Back Stance has the back leg bent
- Make sure to turn over the shoulder of the arm that is out. For instance, to go from move 2 to 3 turn towards the north.
- Target punches to the sternum.

Demo 1

Demonstration 1 includes three basic blocks. Make sure to shift your weight on back stance and shift the focus of your eyes towards where you are blocking.

1. Left Back Stance, Left low block
2. Right Back Stance, Right low block
3. Left Back Stance, Left middle block
4. Right Back Stance, Right middle block

5. Horse stance, left high block
6. Horse stance, right high block
7. Horse stance, left-right double punch

Grappling A and B

A: Falling Technique (from *junbi*): left, right, backwards, forwards
**make sure to tuck your chin to your chest (except when falling forward)
and hit the ground with all parts at the same time.*

Falling techniques come from Judo. The idea behind falling is to
minimize impact upon hitting the ground and to avoid serious
injury. Thus, depending on how high you fall from and onto what
surface, falling may hurt, but you should not break any bones unless
you fall is extreme (i.e, one KAT student fell off his roof onto
concrete, and broke only his ankle) It is important to keep your
head tucked into your chest to avoid hitting your head on the
ground. You should practice falls from a sitting position originally
and then when you get better try from standing. When you stand,
the first thing you do is bend your leg so that you are crouching.

Side Fall-Here you fall on one side of your body. To go to the
right, lift your right leg and grab your left shoulder with your right
arm. On falling, first you touch the right side of your core and then
roll on down the side of your spine. At the moment you hit the
ground, your right leg and right arm should straighten out and hit
the ground. Your arm should be out at about 45 degrees from your
body. The point of this is so that you can spread out the area that
contacts the ground, which reduces the pressure on your body.
Your left knee should be bent so you can get up quickly.

Back Fall-What you do is roll directly backwards and slap both of
your hands at the same time. Make sure to keep that 45 degree
angle, so you look like an arrow and not a cross (90 degree angle
between body and arms).

Front Fall- Here you are going to fall forwards and spread your
legs while landing on the palms of your hands and your forearms,
from the tips of your fingers down to your elbows. Look to the side.
(Do not land on palms of hands only, knifehands, or fists)

B: Rolling Technique (from sparring stance): Forwards and backwards over the left shoulder, switch, forwards and backwards over the right shoulder. Your head should never hit the ground. Rolls should be smooth. When doing backwards rolls, go straight back at first and then go to 45 degrees.

Board Break at test will be Ax Kick.
Kick down hard on the center of the board with your heel.

Basic Postures

Charyut (**Attention Stance**) - Your body is straight with your feet together and your hands in fists at your side. The movement should be accomplished in a split second.

Junbi (**Ready Stance**) – Move your left leg outwards while lifting your open hands to your sternum bring them down to right in front of your waist, close fists, and do not snap. The whole movement takes 5 seconds. Ready your mind as you ready your body.

Kyong Neh (**Bow**) – Bend at the waist to almost 90 degrees and come back up. The whole movement takes 5 seconds.

Terminology Group 1: Basics (White Belts)

Uniform (*Dobok*)	Workout area (*Do Jang*)	Yell (*ki hap*)	At Ease (*Shi Yoh*)
Attention (*Charyut*)	Back to Joon Bi *(Pa Roh)*	Bow (*Kyoung Neh*)	Ready Stance (*Joon Bi*)

White to Yellow Belt Written Test

Congratulations! You are now ready for the test. Fill out this written test and hand it in with your testing application on the day of the test. Don't forget to take pictures at the belt ceremony!

Name: Date:

What are the three components of practicing Taekwondo?

Break down the word *Taekwondo:*

*Tae*_____

*Kwon*_____

*Do*_____

How many moves are in your form Chun Ji?

If you continue to train hard and test when you are eligible, **at what date** will you reach 1st degree black belt? (Belt tests are every three months, with a 6th month wait at 1st *Gup*.)

What does the Korean word *Charyut* mean?

What does the Korean word *Dobok* mean?

What are you most excited to learn about in Taekwondo?

White to Yellow Belt Essay

Word of the Month:_____

Yellow Belt – 9th *Gup*

Yellow Belt Key Points

- Understand the history of Taekwondo and KAT in more detail.
- Start partner practice with One Steps and grappling C/D.
- Keep building basic stances, kicks and hand techniques.

Lesson: History

History of Taekwondo (Adapted from official WTF and ITF histories)

The earliest forms of Korean martial arts reach back roughly 2000 years, although the ancient martial arts were very different from modern Taekwondo. Cave paintings from the *Koguryo* dynasty show sparring postures that were likely linked with religious rituals of the time. The *Silla* dynasty (57 BC-AD 435) saw the birth of the famous *Hwarang* warriors, a military, educational and social organization of noble youths. Their code of honor had five key points that are important to Taekwondo today. These included:

Loyalty to the nation
Respect and obedience to one's parents
Faithfulness to one's friends
Courage in battle and
Avoidance of unnecessary violence and killing.

The influence of the *Hwarang* played an important role in unifying the three kingdoms of ancient Korea. At *Kyongju*, the ancient capital of *Silla*, two Buddhist images are inscribed on the inner walls of *Sokkuram* cave in *Pulkuk-sa* Temple. These two "Diamond Warriors," protecting Buddhism from devils, are the inspiration for the Poomsae *Keumkang*.

The next development in Korean martial arts saw the rise of *Subak*, which was practiced not only as a skill to improve health and as a sport activity, but also encouraged as a martial art during the Koryo dynasty. *Subak* reached its highest popularity during the reign of King *Uijong*, between 1,147 and 1,170 A.D.

Over the next few centuries, there was not much recorded development. The Japanese colonization of Korea was the next major event in the history of Korean martial arts. This thirty-five year occupation lead to many deep feelings of resentment in Korea, as can be seen in the meanings of the International Taekwondo Federation (ITF) forms. The occupation brought the exchange of many ideas, and martial arts was no exception. Towards the end of this occupation many schools, or *kwan*, were established in Korea. On September 16, 1961, the Korea Taekwondo Association was established, in order to unify the *kwans*.

In the 1960's, Korean instructors began going abroad to teach Taekwondo. This could be called a turning point in the history of Taekwondo. 1966 was a pivotal year. In January, Grandmaster Larry McGill started teaching at Metro State University of Denver, making it one of the oldest Collegiate Taekwondo programs in the nation. On March 22nd, the International Taekwondo Federation (ITF) was formed and General Choi Hong Hi was elected president. General Choi was instrumental in spreading Taekwondo across the world with a series of demonstration trips, and he was the one who came up with the name of Taekwondo.

The late 1960s and early 1970s were tumultuous times for Korea in general and Taekwondo in particular. General Choi had a falling out with many of the other masters and in 1972 moved the ITF headquarters from Seoul, Korea to Toronto, Canada. In May 1973, representatives of nineteen countries met in Seoul and established the competing World Taekwondo Federation (WTF). Henceforth, the WTF was to focus more on the sport aspect of Taekwondo, while the ITF was to focus on the more traditional aspect. The world's focus shifted to the WTF, which is more popular and recognized by more international sporting bodies. Over time, the sparring style of the WTF became distinct from Karate and is now properly its own style. In 2017, The World Taekwondo Federation rebranded as World Taekwondo (WT).

WT has a member federation in basically every country (208 members) and the global Taekwondo population is estimated at almost 100 million people. As of 2018, there were 10 million Kukkiwon (black belt) *Dan* rankings awarded worldwide, with 9.1 million in Asia and the majority of those in Korea.

Spurred by the recognition of Taekwondo by the International Olympic Committee (IOC) in 1980, Taekwondo rapidly became an international sport. It was adopted as a demonstration sport in the Seoul Olympics in 1988 and the Barcelona Olympics in 1992. Taekwondo was an official sport at the 2000 Olympics in Sydney, Australia.

US Olympic Medal Winners

	Men	Women
2000	Steven Lopez (Gold, Feather)	
2004	Steven Lopez (Gold, Welter)	Nia Abdallah (Silver, Feather)
2008	Steven Lopez (Bronze, Welter) Mark Lopez (Silver, Feather)	Diana Lopez (Bronze, Feather)
2012	Terrance Jennings (Bronze, Feather)	Paige McPherson (Bronze, Welter)
2016		Jackie Galloway (Bronze, Heavy)

Taekwondo has quickly consolidated its position in the sports world. Aside from the continental championships, World Championships, World Cup Taekwondo, CISM Taekwondo Championships and FISU World University Championships, Taekwondo is being played as an official sport in most international multi-sport games, such as Pan American Games, All Africa Games, Southeast Asian Games and Central American Games.

KAT School History

The Korean Academy of Taekwondo was founded in February of **1980 by Grandmaster Jae Kyu Chung**. Grandmaster Chung trained in Korea and was a member of the Korean Green Berets and won many national and international titles. After leaving Korea, he taught for eight years in Brazil and then came to Colorado. He built up the Aurora school on Alameda St, and then later at 380 S. Potomac St. He also taught at the third building located at 13700 E. Alameda, near Aurora Mall. During this time he was the coach of the US National Taekwondo team.

Grandmaster Chung also built up two sister schools, the Littleton and Arvada branches of the Korean Academy. In the mid-nineties, he transferred control over the Aurora school to his student, **Master Ghassan Timani**. Master Ghassan also had help teaching class from Master Andre Olivera, one of Master Chung's students from Brazil. Eventually, Master Andre left to form his own school.

Master Ghassan continued to exercise control over the Korean Academy, and Grandmaster Chung sold all three of the schools, and he returned to Korea to pursue a career in politics, including serving as the head of security for Kim De Jung, the former president of South Korea.

In the fall of 1998, the third building was torn down to make way for a freeway off ramp and so the school moved again, this time to 16800 E Mississippi.

The school remained in that location for six years until Master Ghassan built a new school across the street. The new building has the significant advantage that it is not part of a complex as other schools are— it is a free standing structure designed from the ground up to provide an intelligent layout, modern safety equipment, and the latest digital media technology.

2004 saw the return of **Master Bill Pottle**, one of the Korean Academy's highest-ranking students. After getting his black belt from KAT, Master Bill trained at Cornell University and the University of Pennsylvania where he was pursuing academic and professional interests. Master Bill also took over the program at Metro State University.

In 2006 the school welcomed many students from the former United Academy of Taekwondo. With the closing of United Academy, KAT also became the oldest Taekwondo school in Aurora.

In 2007 the school took over the former Garrett/Strantz Taekwondo in Littleton, CO, and installed a state of the art 'floating floor' in the facility. KAT expanded again in 2009, taking over the former ML Parr Academy of Taekwondo in Loveland.

The school has also had branches in Baghdad, Iraq (in one of Hussein's former palaces) and Joshua, Texas, through the work of Master Emelio Tio.

The school is now organized as the KAT Network, with 10+ different companies founded by KAT black belts who teach in various elementary schools, gyms, community centers, etc.

Over the years, thousands of students have trained with the Korean Academy. We have had many state, national, and international champions. In all of these years, we have had an excellent safety record.

For a much more detailed, comprehensive and up-to-date account, visit the history section of the KAT website.

Think about how you can make your mark on KAT school history in the future.

School Logo

The KAT logo embodies the philosophy of the school. It is a blend

of traditional symbols and modern materials and rendering. The base of the logo is the Taoist concept called Yin-Yang in Japanese and Um-Yang in Korean. This concept signifies the essential balance in nature between light/dark, day/night, male/female, positive/negative, etc. For our school, it represents our philosophy of '*a mind in the future and a heart in the past.'* The Um-Yang is interrupted to represent the blue sky and snow-capped mountains of Colorado.

The tiger in the middle represents strength, stealth, and explosiveness. It is also a play on the initials of our school.

The three symbols are the Korean words of Tae, Kwon, and Do.

The logo has many forms for different KAT branch locations, programs, and teams within the school. The current logo was made in 2004 by Jason Charles.

Lesson: Stretching
(Adapted from *Taekwondo: State of the Art*)

Flexibility has always been important in Taekwondo, as all our kicks are directed above the belt. It is even more important now that the rules have been changed to award up to four points for a powerful head shot. The main key to flexibility is persistence. Beyond initially learning the correct body alignment, stretching does not require skill. Therefore it is an excellent workout for lower ranks to do. Not only can you do it in just a few minutes without supervision, it will help you to get your other kicking techniques much easier. Set aside ten minutes to stretch every day and you will soon be flexible. There are several important things to remember:

- Your muscles will stretch much easier if they are warm
- Stretch just slightly beyond where it begins to hurt. Going too far will damage your muscles with microtears. When they heal, you will be less flexible than before.
- Unless actually stretching your back, keep it straight. This will provide the proper alignment of your hips and the muscles that attach there.
- Breathe evenly and relax. Inhale through your nose while relaxing and then exhale through your mouth while elongating your muscle.

- The most important thing is being regular. Try to stretch after *every* class or *every* night before you go to sleep.
- If possible, try to multitask your workouts. For example, stretching while watching TV or doing homework is an excellent way to be more efficient.

PNF Stretching- PNF stretching, or Proprioceptive Neuromuscular Facilitation is a way to combine stretching with isometrics in order to achieve better flexibility. The key is that immediately after a contraction, your muscle will relax. You can use this time of relaxation to extend your range of motion. For example, if you stretch to your limit and then push your muscle against something (partner, floor, etc) so that it contracts for 5-10 seconds (isometric contraction), once you release the contraction you will be able to stretch slightly farther.

Yellow Belt Testing Requirements

Taeguek Meanings- The eight Taeguek forms represent the eight (pal) Gwe. This philosophy was first outlined in the ancient Chinese manuscript called "*The Book of Changes.*" It is a Taoist philosophy, that is, it follows Lao Tzu's concepts of Yin and Yang being two equal and opposite balancing forces in the world. From Yin comes Seon, Gam, Gan, and Gon. From Yang comes Jin, Ri, Tae, and Keon. Metaphysically, some are closer to others, and those forms are closer together.

Form 1 - Tae Geuk Il Jang

"**Keon Gwe**" Heaven and light. Beginning with enthusiasm.

Note, the front hand is the same as the front foot unless specified otherwise.

1) Left walking stance low block.
2) Right walking stance middle punch
3) Right walking stance low block
4) Left walking stance middle punch
5) Left long stance low block, right hand middle punch
6) Right walking stance middle block, left hand out to in middle block
7) Left walking stance right hand middle punch
8) Left walking stance middle block, right hand out to in middle block
9) Right walking stance left hand middle punch
10) Right long stance low block, left hand middle punch.
11) Left walking stance high block
12) Front kick, right walking stance punch
13) Right walking stance high block
14) Front kick, left walking stance punch
15) Left long stance low block.
16) Right long stance middle punch, (*kihap*)

Form 1 Key Points

•　　Make sure to step across your body with the **left** foot when coming back from line 3 to line 2.

•　　Make sure not to step too far after the front kicks (walking stance)

•　　Make sure to step **forwards** and drag your foot during moves 5 and 10. You need to move from line 2 to line 3.

Demonstration #2

1. Left back stance, knifehand low block
2. Right back stance, knifehand low block
3. Horse stance, left knifehand high block and right neck strike.
4. Horse stance, right knifehand high block and left neck strike.
5. Horse stance, right hand spear finger strike with support
6. Horse stance, left hand spear finger strike with support
7. Horse stance, right/left double middle punch.

Yellow Belt Grappling Drills

Remember, just because someone WANTS to hurt you doesn't mean that they GET to hurt you. The person who gets to decide is the one who has control. Self-control is one of the most important virtues in martial arts, but the control mentioned here is more of a physical level of control.

C: Standing Control: Try to get to the double underhooks position. The underhook position is the grip that is on the inside. It gives more control as well as the ability to get behind your partner. Do it ten times with little resistance and then go free. Here are the ways to win:

1) **Usual Way** – Lift your partner
2) Get your partner's back.
3) Your partner falls down.
4) A tie goes to the smaller person.

D: Riding the back: Half circle to the right, half circle back, half circle to the left, half circle back, full circle to the right, full circle to the left.

Grappling drill D helps you with balance as well as getting used to someone putting their weight on you. You will see the other part of the drill in grappling 4. When someone tries to tackle you, you can do falling technique on their back (sprawl) and spin around to get back control.

Yellow Belt One Step Sparring

1 (Yellow)	Slide to right side, left knifehand block and right punch to face followed by double punch to the chest all in horse stance. Your feet should be equidistant from theirs.
2 (Yellow)	Slide to right side, left knifehand block and right knifehand attack neck, bring hands and feet in, right knifehand strike to neck with pull, step forward with left foot, trip with right and punch on ground. Ground punch should be executed in long stance
3 (Yellow)	Step in to back stance, right outside to inside forearm block. Just pivot (don't step) and spin to left knifehand strike in crossed stance.

Korean Terminology Group 2: Basics Part 2

Excuse Me (*Shile Hahm Nida*)	Congratulations (*Chook Ha Hahm Nida*)	I am sorry (*Me Ahn Hahm Nida*)	Turn Around (*Deui Ro Dora*)
How are you? (*Ahn Nyoung Ha SeYo?*)	I'm name (name *Em Nida*)	Thank You (*Kam Sa Hahm Nida*)	You are welcome (*Chun Man Aeyo*)

Yellow to High Yellow Belt Written Test

Congratulations! You are ready for your second promotion. Complete this section prior to the test. Don't forget to take pictures at the belt ceremony!

Name: Date:

Name the previous Head Masters of KAT, and the current Head Master of KAT:

What do you need to improve on?

Who are your closest friends in your belt group now?

Which assistant instructor has made the biggest impact on your training?

What does the Korean terminology *Chook Ha Hahm Nida* mean?

What does the Korean terminology *Chun Man Aeyo* mean?

Explain PNF stretching:

Yellow to High Yellow Belt Essay

Word of the Month:_____

High Yellow Belt: 8th *Gup*

High Yellow Belt Key Points

- You can start to attend sparring class to get more realistic practice.
- Get a great handle on basics so you can move on to Level 2 class.
- Work with a resisting partner on grappling drill E.

Lesson: Rank and Titles

Rank has always been an important part of many martial arts systems. Traditionally, the rank in a system was directly correlated with a person's place in society or their rank in the army. Denoting rank by colored belts worn around the waist is a relatively new phenomenon, which has only come about a little more than 100 years ago.

Rank is an important part of Taekwondo culture. When we do many things like line up or compete, rank comes into account. Rank should not be seen as a higher-ranking person "having control" over a lower ranking person, or as a lower ranking person having to serve a higher-ranking person. Rather, rank is a reflection of a person's role and responsibility within the school. Higher ranks (*sohn bae nihms*) have a responsibility to look after lower ranks (*hu baes*) and to teach and guide them. With each passing rank, your responsibility grows as more and more people are lower than you. Rank in Taekwondo is denoted by different colors of belts, but when your belt changes you have to change as well. If everyone were to come to class without their belts, an outside observer should be able to tell whom the higher-ranking students and the leaders are.

Taekwondo ranks start with the ***Gup***, or rank away from black belt. After testing for black belt, the student will automatically receive their first ***Dan*** (degree of black belt).

There is also a **Poom** belt for junior black belts. Once they reach the age of 16, their *Poom* certificate automatically converts to the appropriate *Dan* level. As the black belt rank increases, there is more of an emphasis on teaching and developing Taekwondo and less on individual competition. The rank of 10th *Dan* is reserved for certain special circumstances, at the discretion of the president of the World Taekwondo Federation. You cannot test for it, and it is generally awarded posthumously. Two 10th *Dans* include Juan Antonio Samaranch, who was President of the International Olympic Committee when Taekwondo became an official sport and Pope Francis.

Because the KAT curriculum includes much more than the Kukkiwon curriculum, KAT issues two certificates to students who pass their black belt tests. One certificate comes from the Kukkiwon, and the other from KAT in recognition of work done in grappling, community service, multiple opponent sparring, one step sparring, etc. The Kukkiwon certificate is valid all over the world.

Instructors: Traditionally, all black belts were considered instructors. The limit of instructor training was *"go do to them what was done to you."* KAT recognizes that the skills that make someone a good instructor are often different than the skills that make someone a good black belt. Certainly, instructors need the skills of a black belt. Yet, they also need other skills such public speaking, dealing with conflict, and helping students with learning disabilities.

Accomplishment	English Term	Korean Term
Students	Seniors/Juniors	*Son Bae Nim/ Hu Baes*
Highest Rank in class	Class Leader	*Bang Cha Nim*
1st *Dan* – 3rd *Dan*	Black Belt	*You Dan Ja*
4th *Dan* – 7th *Dan*	Master	*Sa Bum Nim*
8th *Dan* +	Grandmaster	*Kwan Jang Nim*
Level 1 Instructor	Junior Instructor	*Kyo Sa Nim*
Level 2 Instructor	Instructor	*Kyo Sa Nim*
Level 3 Instructor	Senior Instructor	*Kyo Sa Nim*
Current head of KAT school.	KAT Head Master	

Note that there is some disagreement over when to use the titles of Master and Grandmaster instructor. The titles were originally developed in the atmosphere of the large Korean training halls, i.e., *Kwan Jang Nim* literally means "Head of the Kwan," which might encompass several separate buildings. It is more equivalent to "School Head," or "Style Head." Master Bill currently holds the title of *KAT Head Master*, although there are older black belts with higher ranks. The Head Master is generally the owner of the school. We reserve the grandmaster title for students who are 8th *Dan* and above. The Kukkiwon allows 4th *Dan* and above to issue *Dan* ranks for their own students, so this is generally when the master title is used.

The following table shows the official KAT belt rankings.

Belt Color	Rank
White	10th *Gup*
Yellow	9th *Gup*
Green Stripe	8th *Gup*
Green	7th *Gup*
Blue Stripe	6th *Gup*
Blue	5th *Gup*
Red Stripe	4th *Gup*
Red	3rd *Gup*
Black Stripe	2nd *Gup*
Double Black Stripe	1st *Gup*
Black	1st-9th *Dan*

We also use white belts with a yellow, green, blue, red stripe, and red stripe with yellow tape for the Little Tigers Program. These belts are all between white and yellow belt and are used for 3 and 4 year olds or students with disabilities that make earning a yellow belt difficult. Most students will go straight from white to yellow.

Belt Groups

The ideal situation is that groups of people will progress through the ranks together. These will become some of your closest friends in the school. Belt groups should take the initiative to practice and synchronize their requirements outside of class time.

Forms: Levels of Knowing

When can you really say that you 'know' your form? In truth, a form can always be practiced more and learned better. KAT has the following five levels of knowing a form to help you understand where you are and what you need to work on next:

Level 1: You understand a little bit about the form and things like what some of the moves are or what pattern the form makes.

Level 2: You now know all of the moves from beginning to end and can execute them all in sequence.

Level 3: You now can do all the details correctly. This means that you have correct chambering, the path of your moves is correct, the stances have the correct weight distribution, etc.

Level 4: You can now do all of the above and add power as well.

Level 5: You can now do the form so well that it takes on an artistic beauty of its own. Someone watching this form can be inspired deep within.

Most people will never make it to level 5, but everyone should get at least to level 4 before progressing.

Testing Requirements

Tae Geuk Ee Jang (Form 2)

"**Tae Gwe**" Joy. Positive attitude, performed gently but forcefully.

1. Left walking stance, low block.
2. Left long stance, middle punch.
3. Right walking stance, low block
4. Right long stance, middle punch
5. Left walking stance, right out to in middle block
6. Right walking stance, left out to in middle block
7. Left walking stance, low block
8. Front kick, right long stance high punch
9. Right walking stance, low block
10. Front kick, left long stance high punch
11. Left walking stance high block
12. Right walking stance high block
13. (spin step) Left walking stance, right out to in middle block
14. Right walking stance, left out to in middle block
15. Left walking stance, low block
16. Front kick, right walking stance, punch
17. Front kick, left walking stance, punch
18. Front kick, right walking stance, punch. (*kihap*)

Form 2 Key Points

- The hardest part is confusing this with form 1 and doing "Form 1.5"
- Don't take extra steps immediately before kicking
- Watch your stances on the way back – this is one of the more difficult forms to end up in the same place.

Grappling Drill E: Side Controls – Cycle through side control positions in order. Total sequence R1-R2-R3-4-L3-L2-L1-L2-L3-4-R3-R2-R1.

The point of this drill is to get good at holding your partner down from the side. Controlling your partner will make it more difficult for them to hurt you and will allow you to set up submissions later on.

Side Control #1 (Also called simply side control) - Suppose your partner is laying down and you are on his left side. Your right hand should have an underarm control on his left arm. (i.e., underhook) Your left hand just grabs his right arm at the bicep. Your chest should be down on his chest and your right knee should be under his

Side Control #1

shoulder to prevent him from rolling. Your legs should be spread wide to maintain your balance and leverage. Push your weight down on your opponent.

Side Control #2- (Also called Side Mount) The side mount often follows the side control. Here, you place your chest on your partner's chest and should be perpendicular to him. You want to get one arm under his head and your other arm under his far arm. You then clasp your arms together to have a secure lock. He may try to come towards you and hook his leg, in which case you bring your arm out

Side Control #2

and fend off his legs. From the side mount you can mainly apply submissions to your partner's head, neck, and arms. Your body should be perpendicular to his.

Side Control #3 – This is mainly a transitory position, not so useful for holding your partner down. From here it is easy to kick over and go to the front mount. You are facing your partner's legs, opposite of the #1 position. Grab your partner's belt or clothes on the opposite side. Your forearm should be on the ground.

Side Control #3

Side Contol #4

Side Control #4 (Also called North-South Position) - In this position you are facing the opposite direction as your partner. You grab his belt with each hand and put your chest down on your partner's head.

One Step Sparring 4-6

4 (Green Stripe, Green)	Left inside to outside crescent kick to knock hand away, right side kick to sternum.
5 (Green St., Green)	Step in, left back stance left out to in middle block, spinning elbow to temple, right forearm strike trip, punch on ground.
6 (Green St., Green)	Step in to right horse stance, double sided arm break, right elbow w/support, right backfist, left turning palm strike to face.

Terminology Group 3: Numbers

Hana (1)	*Dul* (2)	*Set* (3)	*Net* (4)
Tasut (5)	*Yasut* (6)	*Ilgup* (7)	*Yadul* (8)
Ahope (9)	*Yul* (10)	*Summul* (20)	*So Roon* (30)
Il (1st)	*E* (2nd)	*Sam* (3rd)	*Sa* (4th)
Oh (5th)	*Yook* (6th)	*Chil* (7th)	*Pal* (8th)
Koo (9th)	*Ship* (10th)	*Paek* (100th)	*Chun* (1000th)

High Yellow to Green Belt Written Test

Once you pass your test, you will be an intermediate student and no longer a beginner. Don't forget to take pictures at the belt ceremony!

Name: Date:

What **specific** things have you done since the last test to improve the techniques you needed to?

What do you plan to do in the future to keep improving them?

Explain the meaning of the belt ranks *Gup*, *Dan*, and *Poom*. What is the name (both words) of your current rank?

What does the Korean terminology *Yasut* mean?

With Korean terminology in mind, what will be the name of your next form?

High Yellow to Green Belt Essay

Word of the Month:_____

Green Belt 7th *Gup*

Congratulations on passing your green belt test! You are now an intermediate student and it's time to set your eyes on your next goal, black belt! By earning your green belt, you have proven that you aren't one of those people who give up easily. You understand that things that hold true value take real work over time.

Green Belt Key Points
- You are now eligible to participate in the Future Black Belt program and get your belt on the wall.
- You are now an intermediate student. You should keep refining basics and work on gaining skills in free sparring and free grappling.
- Green belt is a time when a lot of new techniques, classes, and applications open up.

Lesson: Distance AKA, the "Donut of Danger"

Taekwondo has often been called a 'game of distance.' Indeed, a few extra inches can be the difference between a crushing blow and a complete miss. But how can your effective striking distance be measured, visualized, and extended?

A simple geometric approximation of striking distance can be formed by fixing one leg and rotating the other leg around the hip

joint. The farthest point you will be able to hit will be at your hip level. If you raise your leg to hit higher, you will decrease your kicking distance. Thus, you will be able to hit your opponent from farther away if you hit to the height of your own hip. The shape that is made is called a torus, but commonly referred to as a donut.

We will simplify the analysis to two dimensions and take a bird's eye view from the top, looking down on the two competitors. The edges of the circle should be fuzzy, in that a competitor is not able to deliver maximum power at the extreme edge of his range. The inside dots represent the body of the competitor, i.e., if any part of the blue circle touches the red dot, then the blue player is able to score on the red player. In this figure, the competitors are at an *idle distance* in that neither can strike the other. Note that the blue player is taller and thus has a longer range (bigger circle) but that the red player is better able to strike on the inside (smaller inner circle).

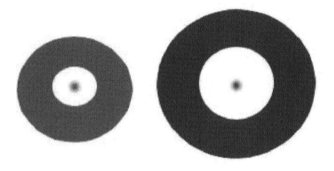

Both players at an *idle distance*

What commonly happens in a sparring match is that both players go to a distance where they can comfortably strike the opposing player, which is usually the *flurry distance*, where both players can strike each other well. In this situation the player who is faster will be able to score more points, although he will have to take significant punishment if the other player is stronger. If one player is faster *and* stronger, then he will be successful as long as he does not stay in his opponent's *optimal distance*.

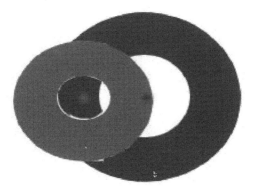

Flurry distance, where both players are capable of hitting each other

It should be obvious that there are two ways to avoid an opponent's kick, moving back and moving in. The white area in the figures is the area where neither player can attack. Often one player will close the distance and end up in a neutral *clinch* position. Clinching can be a useful strategy to disrupt an opponent who is faster or to waste time.

The *clinch* position. The players' chests are touching and neither player can strike the other.

In order to have an advantage, one player must keep the match in his *optimal distance*. This distance varies depending on who has a longer range.

Optimal Distance. The optimal distance is different for the taller blue (left) and the shorter red (right)

As long as there is a difference in range, there is a point where you will be able to strike your opponent and he cannot strike you. This is usually at the outside or inside edge of your range. For example, in the left part of the figure, the blue player positions himself at the outside edge of his range and is able to strike the red player, while the red player is too far away to strike him back. In the right half, the red player goes inside and is able to strike the blue player, while the blue player is too close to strike the red player effectively.

This should lead each competitor to ask 2 fundamental questions:

1. **How can I extend my 'donut of danger'?** – You must extend your effective striking distance both inwards and outwards. The only way to do this is to practice striking targets closer and closer or farther and farther. The kicks change as the distance changes. Crescent kicks are good in the inside, and roundhouse kicks are good to extend distance. Also, the torus was drawn with the hip at a fixed point in space. By moving your hip you can shift your entire torus in that direction. For instance, to hit in a clinch, fold your hips back and you will be able to strike closer to your body.

2. **How can I keep the match at my optimal distance?** The simple answer is that you must have excellent footwork. You must be able to quickly get to the desired position and from there counter your opponent's movements. For example, if you are at your optimal distance and your opponent moves forward, you must move back to keep the distance the same. You must also be able to move laterally and diagonally to cut off distance quickly. The player with the longer range naturally has an advantage because the shorter player will reach his striking distance before he will reach the shorter player's striking distance.

Advanced concepts

Deceptive Range- None of the concepts discussed here are secret, and the strategies are obvious. However, the edges of the donut of danger are different for each player. If you can achieve a longer range than your opponent suspects you may be able to inch into your *optimal distance* while your opponent still believes that you are both in an *idle position*. From there you will be able to strike and surprise him.

Drawing Out Kicks- You will have momentary safety immediately following a kick by your opponent. This is the best time for a shorter player (red) to enter the donut of danger of a larger player (blue). Red can inch into blue's optimal distance and cause blue to strike. Red then slides back and avoids the kick, and then rushes in to strike and take the match to red's optimal distance.

Extending Range with Steps- Although each time a player steps the donuts shift position, if a player steps and strikes immediately, he may be able to extend his range. This holds true for kicks like hop, back leg roundhouse kicks and double kicks.

Letting the Opponent Close Distance- Often it is to the shorter player's advantage to let the tall player close the distance and then counter him. This can negate the taller player's range advantage. This is why back kick is especially necessary for shorter players as they cannot match roundhouse kicks off the line with taller players.

Since the taller player is already coming in, the shorter player can use his back kick and score without having to worry about the distance advantage of the taller player. However, when using a back kick, the shorter player is vulnerable to being faked out by the taller player and countered when he completes his spin.

However, it is important to remember that the player with the shorter range may be able to close the distance, kick, and clinch if he is significantly faster that the taller player. This will work only if the taller player is not good at the *pada chagie*, or receiving kick. If the taller player slides backwards while throwing this kick, he will prevent the shorter player from closing enough distance.

Lesson: Basic Grappling Positions

Grappling drill F covers most of the basic grappling positions. Grappling is similar to football in that both are positional games, but sometimes beginners have trouble because the 'yard markers' are positions instead of numbers. We created this chart to help people understand the different positions and how to move between them. We also put in a few 'touchdowns' (submissions) and the mechanics behind them. Like football, a submission (touchdown) can come from any position, but it is much more likely to happen from a 'good field position.'

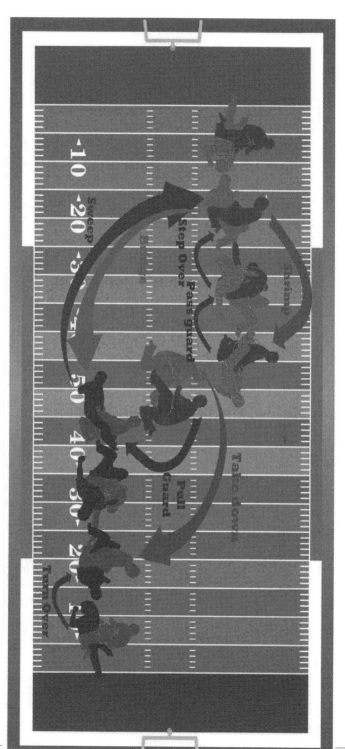

Front Mount- A mount is defined as being on top of the other person and having your legs above their hips. Once you are in the mount, you can easily strike your opponent or apply a submission. The most common submissions from the mount are arm bars and chokes.

Mount

The best way to get out of the mount is not to get into it in the first place. So it is important to remember when you are falling or struggling on the ground that you should get at least one knee up and touching your elbow. Then, you can't be front mounted. Also, whenever you can you should try to hook your legs around your opponent's back. If you can even get one leg around, then you will be in the half guard, which is a completely different story. If you do happen to be mounted though, there are several things you can try. You can try to trap one side and bridge up suddenly, especially when your opponent tries to throw a punch.

You can push his leg down, turn on your side, stick your hips out, and try to hook one of his legs (shrimping). You can try to strike in the groin area, or you can wrap your arms around his back and try to keep your body close enough to his that he cannot strike. You should avoid the natural impulse to turn over on your stomach at all costs as this will put you in a back mount and a much worse position. Grappling drill G covers the main mount escapes.

Secure Mount

The **Secure Mount** is a form of the mount where you wrap your legs around his (grapevine) and put one arm behind his neck and one out, or both out (superman).

The **Secure Mount** is great for holding someone down, but it is difficult for you to apply many submissions or strikes from it.

Back Mount – The back mount is the most dominant position you can have relative to your partner. His neck is open for the most powerful chokes and he cannot see you to defend against your strikes. The main way to escape is by turning into the guard. A variation of the back mount is the **Sitting Back Mount**. Be sure to hook your legs

Back Mount

around the inside of your partner's thighs. Without putting your hooks in, your partner will be able to escape and you will generally not earn points in grappling tournaments.

Sitting Back Mount

Guard – The guard is an important position, especially for the smaller grappler. When you can wrap one or both of your legs around your opponent above the hips, he is in your guard. So, when you are being taken down and cannot mount your opponent, the first thing you should do is to put a good solid guard on.

Guard

You can lock your ankles together to keep yourself in the guard and push your opponent away from you if he tries to punch. If you are able to roll over then you will be in the mount. This type of move is called a sweep. There are many submissions you can apply from the guard, including the guillotine choke, arm bar, kimura lock,

Half Guard

omaplata, and triangle choke when your opponent tries to pass your guard. When your legs are closed and ankles crossed, it's called the **Closed Guard**.

When the legs are open, it's called the **Open Guard**. There are many types of exotic guards like the **Butterfly Guard** (both feet inside opponent's thighs, like the butterfly stretch) **X Guard** (opponent is standing and you cross your legs to trap one of his) **Spider Guard** (grabbing both of your opponent's sleeves and controlling him with the soles of your feet) and **Rubber Guard** (trap your opponent between one arm and one leg).

Butterfly Guard- The butterfly guard is where you are controlling your opponent's arms with your arms and the tops of your feet are inside of his knees or thighs. This position offers possibilities for many sweeps.

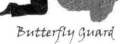

Butterfly Guard

Spider Guard

Spider Guard- This is a variation of the open guard where your feet are on your opponent's thighs or hips. Control your partner's arms with your own.

Testing Requirements

Form 3 – Taeguek Sam Jang
"**Ri Gwe**" Fire and Sun. Passion.

1. Left walking stance, low block.
2. Front snap kick, right long stance, right-left double punch.
3. Right walking stance, low block.
4. Front snap kick, left long stance, left-right double punch.
5. Left walking stance, right knifehand strike to neck.
6. Right walking stance, left knifehand strike to neck
7. Left back stance knifehand middle block
8. (Step out) Right long stance middle punch
9. Right back stance knifehand middle block
10. (Step out) Left long stance middle punch
11. Left walking stance, right out to in middle block
12. Right walking stance, left out to in middle block
13. (spin step). Left walking stance, low block
14. Front kick, right long stance, right left double punch.
15. Right walking stance, low block
16. Front kick, left long stance, left right double punch.
17. Left walking stance, low block, right punch
18. Right walking stance, low block, left punch
19. Front kick, left walking stance, low block, right punch
20. Front kick, right walking stance, low block, left punch, (*kihap*)

Form 3 Key Points
- Make sure to always punch with the front hand first on the double punches.
- Again, the most difficult part is "cross confusing" this form with form 1 and 2, especially on the way back.
- Make sure your long stances on the second line aren't too wide, or you will end behind your mark.

Demonstration Move #3
1. Circle around, left back stance, low guarding block (hands parallel)
2. Circle around, right back stance, low guarding block (hands parallel)

3.　　Left long stance, knifehand high block and neck strike (ITF Turn – step with left leg first)
4.　　Right long stance, knifehand high block and neck strike.
5.　　Horse stance, right hand out to in middle block with support
6.　　Horse stance, left hand out to in middle block with support.
7.　　Right-Left double punch and *kihap*.

Grappling Drill F: Basic Grappling Positions

From GUARD POSITION #1, let partner break your posture.
Change to GUARD POSITION #2.
Go back to POSITION #1 using GUARD POSITION #3.
Open guard with KNEE ON TAILBONE and pass the guard with UNDERHAND GUARD PASS.
Get to FRONT MOUNT - SECURE MODE using by driving knee over
Change to FRONT MOUNT-ATTACK MODE.
Apply FOREARM CHOKE or BOTHER FACE and let partner turn to his/her side to stand up.
Put in BACK MOUNT and roll 360 to one side.
Roll 180 to the other side to SITTING BACK MOUNT.
Let partner undo one hook and TURN INTO GUARD

Posture and balance is very important. When in your partner's guard, the better your posture/base, the more difficult it will be for him to tip you over. Guard Position #1 is a good base with elbows dug into thighs, Guard Position #2 is protecting your neck with both arms extended. Guard Position #3 is keeping your weight down and hands on their biceps.

Terminology Group 4: Applications

Breaking (*Kyuk Pa*)	Meditation (*Mook Nyeom*)	Technique (*Gi Sool*)	Sparring (*Kye Roo Ki*)
One Step (*Il Bo*)	One Step Sparring (*Il Bo Dae Ryun*)	Forms (*Poomsae* (WTF) or *Hyung (ITF)*)	Exercise (*Un Dong*)

Green to High Green Belt Written Test

Name: Date:

What are your strongest and weakest points in grappling?

Who is in your belt group now?

Pick one of your junior belts and explain what you have done to help this person along.

Explain the 'Donut of Danger.'

What does the Korean terminology *Poomsae* mean?

What does the Korean terminology *Mook Nyeom* mean?

From your Korean terminology, what is your favorite part of Taekwondo (in Korean)?

Green to High Green Belt Essay

Word of the Month:_____

High Green Belt 6th *Gup*

Congratulations on passing your test! In some ways, you are entering a dangerous time in your training. Things aren't as 'new and shiny' as they were when you were a yellow belt, yet black belt still seems so far away. There is also the fact that your horizons are expanding and you are realizing just how much there is out there to learn. It can all be a little daunting.

The key is to focus on what is in front of you and just taking one step at a time. Remember, if you *do what you should do* at each belt, you will *be able to do what you should be able to do* at each belt. You might think that you will never be as fast and strong and confident as the black belts, but you will get there. Trust in the system, because it has worked for decades.

High Green Belt Key Points

• Now is a great time to join the future black belt program and get your belt on the wall.

• You should work on free sparring and free grappling techniques with increasing resistance from your partners.

• Start thinking about what type of black belt you will become.

Lesson: Sparring Introduction

(With contributions from Master Tanya Paterno)

Master Tanya Paterno is a forth degree black belt and former MVP of Cornell Taekwondo who has won numerous medals at the Collegiate National Championships, US National Championships, and US Open, and was the first person to win four consecutive spots on the INCTL All Star Team.

Taekwondo sparring is an exciting form of competition. Although the fundamentals are simple, it takes many years of dedicated practice and conditioning to master them. What follows is not a comprehensive guide on how to spar, but some general tips that can come in handy in certain situations.

The basic point of sparring is to score more points than your opponent. Read through the full competition rules to understand how to play the game, especially as there are small changes every few years. Points come from either attacks or counter attacks. The natural stance, or sparring position, faces sideways. This leads to two basic positions in sparring, **open stance** and **closed stance**. In open stance, both competitors have their *hogus* facing the same direction. The name comes from the fact that both are open to a rear leg roundhouse kick. Closed stance is the opposite, where both *hogus* are facing in opposite directions. Knowing which stance you are in is important as certain techniques will work differently depending how your opponent is standing.

There are several kicks and exchanges that you must be familiar with. For example, from open stance, back kick counters roundhouse kick. From closed stance, back leg roundhouse kick counters back leg ax kick. You must drill these until they become like reflexes. Once you become proficient at the basics of attacking and counter attacking, you should start to add in trickery. Each match is a physical battle, but it is also a mental battle. You have to think and guess ahead at what your opponent is going to try to do. Similarly, you should try to lead your opponent in a certain way. Showing your kicks ahead of time by changing your position or shifting your weigh is called *telegraphing*. Look to see if your opponent is showing something. Usually this occurs in more inexperienced sparrers. Learn to hide your next movements. Clear your mind— if you don't know what you are going to do, your opponent won't either. At the same time, learn to intentionally show something in order to draw your opponent to react. This is called faking or trapping. The point of faking is to draw your opponent to counter, and then to recounter his counter. For instance, player A might notice that player B wants to throw a back kick. So player A might fake a roundhouse kick to the open side, and let player B throw his back kick. Then, player A might recounter with a roundhouse kick. However, to go one more level if the same thing happened again player B might fake that he was faked out, and when player A recounters with the roundhouse kick, player B might have the back kick ready again. Usually, there will be only 1 or 2 levels in the attacks and counter attack game, but at the most you should think three moves ahead.

Managing the time and the ring are also important. Always know how many rounds (3 or 2) you are sparring and how long they are. Do not be impatient and rush it to attack if the time is not right. Think through your attacks and what you are going to do. If you have four or six minutes to spar, don't become impatient and throw a match's worth of attacks in the first minute.

Most matches will have electronic scoring. In this case, you can see how both the time and the score are progressing throughout the match. If you are nearing the end of a match and know that you are ahead in points, you can protect your lead. You can wait for you opponent to attack, then counter. Do not sit dormant, but it is not urgent for you to attack to score. Be on the lookout for head shots, which are a fast way to make up points when time is short. Head shots are worth three points but are not allowed for all divisions. Generally only 14 and above black belts (and sometimes adult color belts) will be allowed full head contact. Others will be allowed no head contact (kids) or light head contact.

Always know where you are in the ring. Try not to be forced into a corner. This would be valuable to your opponent in that he now has two choices. He can attack you without you having the ability to move away, or he can force you out of bounds resulting in a penalty against you. If you find yourself caught in a corner it is important to know how to clinch and circle around, thereby getting out of the corner and maybe even forcing your opponent into the corner. Some matches will have square rings and some will have octagonal rings.

Punching is a valuable way to disrupt your opponent's flow of attack. This disruption might be short, but it is enough time for you to throw a kick or two and possibly score. Be sure that you punch, and don't push with an open hand. A punch can score a point if it is hard enough and clear enough.

When you are sparring, you will want to recognize if your

opponent is taller or shorter than you are. If they are shorter than you are, it is in your advantage to be farther away from them. Therefore, you can be at a distance to score, but out of their range to hit you. If they are taller than you are, you should try to be closer, thereby again out of their range to score. One way of doing this is to clinch. Regardless of size, there is an 'idle position' where neither of you can score off the line. Learn how to recognize this distance.

Another important concept to understand is that of acceleration. Acceleration is defined as the change in velocity, which can either be speeding up or slowing down, or a change of direction. Constant speed can be timed easily, even if the speed is fast. In order to confuse your opponents, you must learn how to change your speed. A slow switch could cause your opponent to relax just enough that you can throw a fast roundhouse kick immediately afterwards and they might not have time to recover and then respond to your attack. Similarly, if you can move in directly on your opponent but then slide to the side at the last second, you may be able to cause him to counter your original motion and then you will be able to recounter successfully.

Taekwondo is currently changing rules with respect to things like the use of video replay, coach's challenge cards, and the use of electronic body protectors. With the electronic protectors, you kick your opponent and if it is hard enough (and contact is made with the sock) a point will automatically go up on the scoreboard. You will likely use several different ways when sparring in the dojang, sparring in local tournaments, or competing in the national championships. The KAT competition team class will prepare you well by always staying up to date on the latest rules and technology.

Three Main Types of Techniques

Attacking - The first type of techniques developed were attacking techniques. On a low level of sparring, both players will attack each other and whoever attacks stronger will win.

Counterattacking – Soon, people started developing

counterattacking techniques. This way, you can still defeat someone who is a better attacker than you by either avoiding his kick and coming back with your own or by counterattacking simultaneously.

Trapping – Once both players develop good counterattacks, the match can be very boring as both just stand there because neither wants to attack the other. This brought on the need for trapping techniques. The idea here is to call your partner to attack by *'making him an offer he can't refuse.'* You then apply your counterattack. All traps must have an illusion of safety, a bait (cheese), and a hammer. In sparring, the bait is yourself, or the perceived ability to score on you and the hammer is your counterattack. It's important to note that traps can be defeated by speed. The worst thing is to set out a trap and have a fast mouse come in and take the cheese and escape before the hammer comes down. The more experienced your opponent is, the more likely it is that they will know you are trying to trap them, and the larger 'cheese' you will have to put in your trap.

In general, someone who attacks a lot will lose to someone who is patient and counterattacks, and someone who likes to do a lot of counterattacks will be defeated by someone with good trapping skills. In practice, a good competitor will need to be proficient at all three sets of skills.

Sparring Stance (By Master Matthew Bailey)

Master Matthew Bailey is a 5ᵗʰ degree black belt and has been with the KAT for most of his life. He formerly served in the US Air Force and represented the United States Armed Forces in Taekwondo at the World Military Championships. He is currently certified by USAT at the highest coaching level available and is a coach of the KAT competition team.

The definition of a good sparring stance is the body position which allows any tactical or technical advantage for the competitor. All actions progress from this stance. The question to know is which is the best stance? The answer is quite difficult as there is not any one stance for every athlete. It can vary according to each person's specifics, for instance, mood, behavior, and strategy. Even though it's not necessary to impose a definite position, here are a few basic principles:

    -The space between the feet should not be excessive, just about shoulder-width distance apart.
    -The body needs to be loose and fluid, to allow springing off the feet in order to attack quickly while maintaining balance.
    -Slightly bending your knees with the weight on the lead leg will allow for quicker movement.
    -The shoulders should be loose with the arms minimally contracted, to allow you to attack quickly.
    -A longer stance can create a longer distance between you and your opponent.
    -Make sure that you don't telegraph your kicks by the way you position your body.

Testing Requirements

Form 4 – Tae *Geuk* Sa Jang
"**Jin Gwe**" Thunder. Troublesome times require a sound mind to overcome them.

1.   Left back Stance, knifehand guarding block
2.   (fold down) Right long stance, spearfingers strike with support.
3.   Right back Stance, knifehand guarding block
4.   (fold down) Left long stance, spearfingers strike with support.
5.   Left long stance, right knifehand neck strike, left high block.
6.   Front kick, right long stance, left middle punch.
7.   Left side kick, right side kick, back stance guarding block.
8.   Left back stance, turning middle block
9.   Front kick, return to left back stance, right out to in middle block.
10.   Right back stance, turning middle block
11.   Front kick, return to right back stance, left out to in middle block.
12.   Left long stance, right knifehand neck strike, left high block.
13.   Front kick, right long stance, front backfist to face.

14. Left walking stance, left out to in middle block, right punch
15. Right walking stance, right out to in middle block, left punch
16. Left long stance, out to in middle block, right/left double punch.
17. Right long stance, out to in middle block, left/right double punch. *(kihap)*

Form 4 Key Points

• This form introduces several timing issues. Make sure to finish your hand techniques and stances at the same time. This is particularly true after each kick.

• All blocks happen with the ulna bone (pinkie side)

• The 'flow' at the end of the form is really nice!

Grappling Drill G: Mount Escapes:

1. From being mounted, SHRIMP to guard and do SCISSOR SWEEP.
2. Let partner do the same.
3. Afterwards, trap one side and BRIDGE.
4. Open the guard with STAND UP GUARD OPEN and use LEG TOSS GUARD PASS to side control #2.
5. Move to front mount.
6. Let your partner bridge you.
7. Let partner use stand up guard open to open your guard, then use THIGH-SIT SWEEP to mount him.
8. Let partner put in guard and let him push you away to perform PROPER STANDING.

Adults and black belt candidates do the full drill. Children just do the three key moves.

Shrimping - Shrimping means to basically slide out of your partner's mount. Of course, if you move by yourself then they can move with you, so you need to block their knee with your elbow. This move is also sometimes called elbow/knee escape. This move gets its name because on the top view you look like a shrimp with your back curved.

Bridging – In bridging you roll over and end up in your partner's guard. The key is that you first have to trap the arm and leg of the side you want to go to in order to stop them from defending your bridge.

Proper Standing – When humans normally stand up, we do it like a helicopter (vertically). This won't work when someone is close enough to hit you or push you back over. In this drill, you will stand up like an airplane (with a runway). Basically, you push off one leg and jump backwards while standing.

One Step Sparring

7 (Blue Stripe, Blue)	Step in to right back stance, turn back side, left elbow w/ support, left backfist to face, left hammerfist to groin (or groin grab and throw).
8 (Blue Stripe, Blue)	Step out to left long stance while ducking under the punch and do right ridge hand to sternum, right backfist, left ridge hand, both to temple. Turn hips on the last strike.
9 (Blue Stripe, Blue)	Step in and right outside to inside middle block with foot stomp, duck, grab opponent's right leg and pull to trip, pull leg and left heel strike to groin.

Terminology Group 5: Around the Dojang (High Green Belts)

Color Belts (*Hu Dan Ja*)	Black Belt (*You Dan Ja*)	Class Leader- (*Ban Chang Nim*)	Instructor (*Kyo Sa Nim*)
Master (*Sa Bum Nim*)	Grand Master (*Kwon Chang Nim*)	Junior Belt (*Hu Bae*)	Senior Belt (*Sohn Bae Nim*)

Bow to class leader (*Bang Chang Nim Kye Kyoung Net*)
Bow to instructor (*Sa Bum Nim Kye Kyoung Net*)

High Green to Blue Belt Written Test

Congratulations! You've managed to make it to the halfway point to black belt. Now is the time to intensify your training. Don't forget to take pictures at the belt ceremony!

Name: Date:

Board Break: Back Kick

What are your goals for Taekwondo now?

Who is in your belt group now? How have you helped each other to make it this far?

Has your ability to concentrate and focus improved since taking Taekwondo?

What are the three main types of Sparring Techniques?

Explain how to spar someone who is tall and has a good *pada chagie.*

What does the Korean terminology *Sohn Bae Nim* mean?

What does the Korean terminology *Kwon Chang Nim* mean?

From your Korean terminology, how do you say, "Bow to Instructor" (in Korean)?

High Green to Blue Belt Essay

Word of the Month:_____

Blue Belt 5th *Gup*

Congrats! You are now at the halfway point (numerically) between white and black belt. Of course, the belt rack is not to scale! You need to work even harder to achieve your goals.

Blue Belt Key Points

- Avoid the *'Blue Belt Blues'* – Things aren't 'new and shiny' anymore and but black belt can still feel far away. Keep working hard!
- The number of previous requirements can grow quickly. Make sure to spend some time on them to keep up.
- 11 Year olds and up can be invited to the Assistant Instructor program. Contact Master Bill or your main instructor if interested.

Lesson: Path of Instructors

In a certain sense, all of us are both students and teachers. However, KAT has formalized a training for instructors to grow and develop their careers.

KAT Assistant Instructors - Once you are 11 years old and a blue belt you can be invited to Assistant Instructor Training. Assistant Instructors help with a certain aspect of a class, like group training or warmup. You will need to pass the test and become certified in CPR and First Aid.

KAT Instructors – Once you are 16 and High Red Belt, you can become an official KAT Instructor. You can teach classes at the dojang under supervision, or teach your own classes (once 18)

KAT Network Owner – KAT Instructors can also create their own separate company and become part of the KAT Network.

Lesson: Physiology of Submissions

There are many different submission holds that you can apply on your partner. A good general rule is that the bigger and stronger your opponent, the smaller the part of their body you should attack. The point of a submission is to force your partner to give up by causing them pain or by achieving a position that could cause them permanent injury unless they yield.

All submissions require first fixing your partner's body and then forcing movements that are outside of the normal range of motion or putting pressure that causes pain.

Joint Locks – A very common submission is to pick a joint and force it to move in an unnatural way. A clear understanding of human physiology is thus critical to understanding why joint locks can succeed. Hinge joints (elbow and knee) are vulnerable to hyperextension, which is straightening the arm or leg farther than it can normally go. The ball and socket joints of the hip and shoulder can be used in submissions that rotate the leg or arm. In general, nearly every joint can be locked. **Do not** use any submissions that manipulate any of the joints in the spine. **Do not** use any submissions that turn the knee. These two types of submissions are dangerous and not allowed to be used in KAT.

Pressure Points – You can also force your partner to tap by applying pressure to a muscle (bicep cutter), tendon (Achilles lock), or nerve. These submissions generally require locking up the partner so they cannot simply twist out.

Physiology of Choking

Choking is a very powerful technique that can enable a smaller person to completely subdue a larger one. However, if done improperly or held for too long, choking can lead to serious injuries or even death. Still, choking is usually considered a more humane response in self-defense situations because it generally causes less damage to an opponent than striking and does not give a concussion like a knockout does.

It is important to understand what a choke is and how it works. Everyone should read the excellent information at The Judo Info Page (www.judoinfo.com/chokes.htm)

Physiologically, a choke is cutting off oxygen to the brain. Normally, a person breathes in air into their lungs. Blood comes into the lungs from the left side of the heart, where it becomes filled with oxygen. It then returns to the right side of the heart, where it goes through the aorta to the rest of the body. There are four main ways to interrupt this process.

Carotid Chokes – Carotid chokes, or blood chokes, technically called strangulation techniques, cut off the flow of oxygenated blood to the brain by putting pressure on both of the carotid arteries. This type of choke is the quickest, easiest, and most effective way to cut off oxygen to the brain.

Windpipe Chokes – Windpipe chokes, or air chokes, cut off air to the lungs. These type of chokes take longer to work because there is still some air left in the lungs and some oxygenated blood in the heart that will still reach the brain. However, usually the opponent will tap out due to pain on the trachea before losing consciousness.

Constriction Techniques – The third way to deprive the brain of oxygen is to put pressure on the opponent's chest so that their lungs cannot expand. This type of attack is rarely successful for a smaller person against a bigger person, but can be helpful as a way to tire your opponent in a long match. In this case, you will make his muscles fatigue more easily as you deprive them of oxygen. They may not tap from this technique, but it will make your other attacks more successful.

Smothering Techniques – The last, and least direct and effective method, is to smother your opponent by covering his mouth and nose with a part of your body. Again, this will not often make your partner tap out, but it can be effective in causing your partner to commit. For example, if his arms are locked tightly together, you may cover his mouth and nose so he will have to unlock his arms to defend. When he does so, you can go for arm bar.

Regardless of what type of choke is applied, here is what will happen: After the hold is sunk in, the person being choked may begin to feel pain or dizzy. At this point, students should immediately tap out and the partner will relax the hold.

If the choke continues beyond this point, 5-15 seconds later the person being choked will fall unconscious. When choking a partner, it is extremely important to watch for signs of unconsciousness and release immediately.

KAT students should make every effort to release chokes before unconsciousness. Although unconsciousness may occur and is considered safe, these situations should be very rare.

If the choke is released, the person should regain consciousness normally within 20 seconds with no long term adverse effects. You may gently shake or massage them to help increase the blood flow. If they do not regain consciousness within 20 seconds, seek immediate medical attention.

If for some reason the choke were to continue after the other person is unconscious, serious damage would result in a manner of minutes. There is some debate in the scientific community on exactly when brain damage occurs, but it is somewhere between 5 and 15 minutes of unconsciousness caused by lack of oxygen in the brain. Brain death will occur shortly after.

It is extremely important when applying submission holds to understand how to tap before damage is done. You will usually feel pain before injury. Also, when applying a submission hold, it is critical to monitor your partner carefully. Someone on the street may not understand about tapping, and may want to give up. Always apply less pressure rather than more when unsure. Also, although submissions should be set up or 'sunk' quickly, the pressure should be applied gently and slowly. **Unlike most techniques, students should do submissions only in the school and not practice them at home**.

Arm Bar - In the arm bar you are trying to hyperextend the elbow. You want to get your hips close to their body and turn the arm so that the elbow is hyperextended. This works great from the mount, guard, and back.

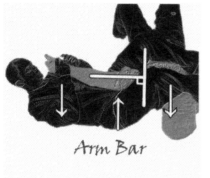

Arm Bar

Arm Bar from Guard

To defend, turn into your partner's arm bar and grab both of your hands together and bend your arm. This will protect you only for a few seconds. Switch your hips and walk into the arm bar, stacking him so that he cannot extend his hips. Walk around to gain side control or go into your partner's guard. When doing arm bar from the guard, push up with your hips (the arrow would be coming out of the page)

Bent Arm Arm Bar- This name is somewhat deceptive as the joint being locked is the shoulder. It mostly works from the mount. You should pretend that you are cleaning their knuckles on the floor.

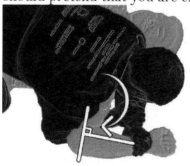

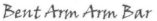

Bent Arm Arm Bar

Kimura

Kimura Lock – The Kimura lock is named after a famous martial artist. It is a shoulder lock similar to the bent arm bar. Kimura locks can be effectively applied from the guard, side control, and #4 positions.

Blue Belt Grappling Techniques

1. **Defense against a tackle.** Alex rushes at Bob to take him down. Bob falls backwards and crosses his hand over. Bob puts in his guard and then applies GUILLOTINE CHOKE. Bob reaches around and applies KIMURA LOCK. Bob does HIP BUMP SWEEP to get into the mount position and raises his fist.

2. **Defense against a boxer.** Alex comes at Bob with several punches. Bob dodges until he finds a good punch and does DOUBLE LEG TAKEDOWN to the mount. Alex again punches on the ground and Bob catches the arm and applies BENT ARM BAR and then transitions to ARM BAR.

The blue belt grappling techniques switch from letters to numbers, and from simple positional skills to common scenarios which progress to submissions. Again, care should be taken to use resistance.

For grappling 1, make sure not to hit your partner's head on the ground when falling into your guard.

For grappling 2, make sure to have good boxing technique and also to shoot fully for double leg. Timing is key – you must shoot when they are coming forward.

Demonstration #4

1. Horse stance, scissors block (left middle, right low.)
2. Horse stance, scissors block (right middle, left low)
3. Horse stance, right vertical punch with support
4. Horse stance, left vertical punch with support
5. Horse stance, right palm strike to face and left high block
6. Horse stance, left palm strike to face and right high block
7. Horse stance, right left double punch.

Form 5 - *Tae Geuk Oh Jang*

"Seon Gwe" Wind. Deadly, but also gentle and repetitious

1. Left long stance, forearm low block.
2. Left stance, hammerfist.
3. Right long stance, forearm low block.
4. Right stance, hammerfist.
5. Left long stance, left out to in middle block, right out to in middle block.
6. Front kick, right long stance front backfist, left out to in middle block.
7. Front kick, left long stance front backfist, right out to in middle block.
8. Right long stance, front backfist.
9. Left back stance, knifehand middle block
10. Right long stance, turning elbow strike.
11. Right back stance, knifehand middle block
12. Left long stance, turning elbow strike.
13. Left long stance, low block, right out to in middle block
14. Front kick, right long stance, low block, left out to in middle block.
15. Left long stance, high block
16. Right side kick and hammerfist, right long stance, left elbow smash.
17. Right long stance, high block
18. Left side kick and hammerfist, left long stance, right elbow smash.
19. Left long stance, low block, right out to in middle block.
20. Front snap kick, stomp, back cross stance right backfist.

Form 5 Key Points
- The 2nd and 4th moves use Left Stance and Right Stance. This is the only time those two stance are used in any form.
- On steps with multiple hand techniques, do the first one with the stance, and the others shortly after.
- This is a 'big' form. There are no walking stances!

Korean Terminology Group 6: Sparring Match (Blue Belts)

Begin (*Si Jak*)	Blue (*Chung*)	Red (*Hung*)	Chest Protector (*Ho Gu*)
Win (*Seung*)	Continue (*Kye Soke*)	Enter (*Ip Chang*)	Penalty (*Gam Jang Hana*)
Injury Time (*Shi Gan*)	Match Time (*Kyeshi*)	End of Round (*Keu Man*)	

Blue Belt to High Blue Belt Written Test

Name: Date:

What kind of Taekwondo practice do you do outside of class?

How has having Taekwondo helped you in life?

Who is in your belt group now?

If you continue to train hard and test when you are eligible, you will reach 1st degree black belt in about one year. What are you doing to prepare for this?

What are the strongest and weakest points of your teaching skills?

What should you do after your opponent 'taps out'?

What does the Korean terminology *Gam Jang Hana* mean? And what could warrant getting one in a match?

What does the Korean terminology *Chung* and *Hung* mean?

From your terminology, how do you say, "Chest Protector" (in Korean)?

Blue Belt to High Blue Belt Essay

Word of the Month:_____

High Blue Belt 4th *Gup*

Congratulations! You are now at a great time in your training where you have time to refine basics before your black belt test. Start to visualize. What will the test be like? Where will you sign your name on the black belt flag?

High Blue Belt Key Points
- You should be starting to think about your black belt test, which could happen in a minimum of about a year.
- You should be gaining skills in free grappling and free sparring
- Continue to focus on basics and practice previous forms regularly.

Lesson: Basic Martial Arts Physics

Sometimes the phrase 'Martial Art' can be misleading, since in the modern area there has been more of an emphasis on science than art. Certainly, the art aspect is still very important in Taekwondo. However, science tends to dig to a deeper level. One can appreciate the work of an artist without knowing exactly how the artist has put together his creation. With science, we search out the fundamental natural principles. For example, one might say *"That is a beautiful kick"* and appreciate the movement. The scientist would ask *"What specific things about that kick make it beautiful?"* and then when he discovers them, think how he can apply what he has learned towards making other kicks beautiful in the same way.

It is important to study physics in order to understand the basis behind Taekwondo techniques. It is important to study math in order to understand physics. One important kind of math to study is calculus. Although it sounds difficult, there are two main important concepts to learn.

The derivative- $\partial y/\partial x$ - The derivative is just a fancy way of looking at how something changes with respect to something else. So, the above equation is basically just saying the change in y divided by the change in x. Often time (t) is substituted for x. For example, the change in position divided by the change in time is known as velocity, or speed.

The Integral- $\int y$ – The integral is the opposite of the derivative. It usually has limits applied to the top and bottom of the $\int$ and it is basically saying to add up the small contributions of some part to the whole over those limits. It's also known as the 'area under the curve.' For example, to find your body mass, you'd take the integral over the shape of your body of the contribution of each infinitesimally small area of your body. Basically, add up the mass of every cell in your body to find the total mass.

Now that we got the calculus out of the way, let's go on to some basic physical quantities.

- **Mass [kg]** = The weight of an object divided by gravity.

- **Force [n]** = The ability to move a mass.

- **Energy [j]** = The ability to do work

- **Position [m]** = The location of an object

Notice that the letter in brackets [] states how each quantity is measured. Mass is in **kilograms**, force is in **Newtons**, energy is in **Joules**, and position is in **meters**. Most of the names of units come from famous scientists.

We must be careful here because in Taekwondo we often think of someone as having a forceful kick. But we usually don't mean this in the same way physicists mean it.

Let's see what happens when we start applying derivatives to those four fundamental concepts. Let's start with position.

First let's see how something's position changes with time, $\partial P/\partial t$.

As stated above, we see that this is the object's velocity. An important thing to note about velocity, however, is that it is a vector so it has two components, magnitude and direction. Thus, something can change its velocity by speeding up or slowing down, or by going at the same speed in a different direction.

- **Velocity [m/s]** = Change in position over time. $V = \partial P / \partial t$

Now what happens if we take the derivative again? Acceleration is the term for how fast something's velocity changes. Again, this can be a change in magnitude or direction. Acceleration is a key component in martial arts. If someone is fast, but fast all the time, then the opponent will be able to time them. If someone can change their speed or direction quickly, then they will be very difficult to beat.

- **Acceleration [m/s²]** = Change in velocity over time. $A = \partial V / \partial t$

In order to find an object's velocity, we can integrate the acceleration over time. We can integrate again (the velocity) to find an object's position.

If we do the same thing with energy, we find that the change in energy with respect to time is called Power. But the change in energy is also referred to the as Work, so we get two definitions for Power.

- **Power [j/s or w]** = Change in Energy over time. $P = \partial E / \partial t$

Power is measured in Watts where one Watt equals one Joule/second.

But what do we mean when we say that someone's kick is powerful? We need a few more concepts to explain what happens when someone strikes another person. There are two critical things that happen- **a transfer of momentum** and **a transfer and dissipation of energy.**

The first important concept in collisions is called momentum. Momentum is what is transferred from one body to another when they run into each other. The other important thing to note is that **Momentum is always conserved**. This means that all of the Momentum transferred from one body is absorbed by the other body.

- **Momentum [kg m/s]** = Mass times velocity m*v

In a collision, we have that the Force equals the change in Momentum divided by the change in time, or $F=\partial M/\partial t$. This leads us to the second important concept, called Impulse. The Impulse is simply the Momentum delivered in a specific time.

- Impulse [kg m/s²] = Momentum delivered in a specific time. $M*\partial V/\partial t$

As you can see from above, $\partial V/\partial t$ is really Acceleration, so this can also be stated as F=MA. In fact, this is known as Newton's Second Law. All Momentum is delivered only if the two bodies are allowed to remain in contact for an infinite amount of time. For our purposes, when hitting another person, we have only a short amount of time in which to transfer our momentum.

The next critical point is that of the transfer and dissipation of energy. There are many different kinds of energy. You have potential energy due to gravity and the chemical bonds in your body. You have energy stored in your muscles like a spring. But the most important for Taekwondo is your Kinetic Energy. This is just a fancy way of saying that your foot has energy because it is in motion.

- **Kinetic Energy [j]** = Energy of a moving object $1/2mv^2$

Just like momentum, **Energy is conserved**. It may change forms, sometimes to unusable forms like heat and sound, but it will not be totally lost.

What happens when one person strikes another?

There are two main kinds of kicks, **pushing kicks** and **snapping kicks**. Pushing kicks include linear kicks like cut kick, and front kick and back kick can also be done in a pushing way. Even roundhouse kick can be done to push, although this is rare. In pushing kicks, the main purpose is to move the other person's body. Thus, the main equation is F=MA. You are trying to apply a Force in order to cause the other person's body to undergo an Acceleration. What happens if the other person is big? M will be large and then that will make A small. This just proves what you already know, that if you kick a bigger person they will not go as far. However, because of the concept of impulse, if you are in contact with the person for a shorter time (lower t) there will be a larger change in (MV). Thus, hitting for a shorter time will let you move someone farther.

Pushing kicks are not done to score, and the main scoring kicks are snapping kicks. In these kicks you are transferring momentum to the opponent and also transferring energy. Here the physics term Power comes in as the amount of Energy we can transfer in a specific time. Energy transfer is what is really important in snapping kicks, especially roundhouse kick. When your foot is in contact with a person, the Kinetic Energy from your foot is transferred to their chest protector. Some of this energy is transferred to heat energy, some is transferred to sound energy, and some penetrates into their body. Energy is the physical force that is responsible for causing damage, not Force or Momentum. Energy is also the physical quantity responsible for breaking boards.

To move a target, kick with your knee bent to transfer force. To damage a target, kick with your knee straight to transfer energy.

In a kick like a back kick, momentum transfer plays a larger role. In this case if the opponent is coming in, the change in momentum is greater because you add together the momentum of his body and the momentum of your kick.

But what does this all tell us? First of all, from the Kinetic Energy equation we see that the Velocity term is squared. So Velocity has a much bigger effect on Energy transferred that mass. Say you increased the mass three times. The kinetic energy would increase by three times. But if you increased the Velocity by three times, the

Kinetic Energy would increase by 9 (3^2) times!

This helps explain why people with long legs seem to be able to score so much easier. We didn't state it before, but the Velocity in that equation is the Instantaneous Linear Velocity. That means the speed that the foot is going right at the moment that it hits the chest pad, in the direction going into the chest pad. Your leg can be considered like the radius of a circle that is swept out in your roundhouse kick. Angular Velocity is how fast something goes around in a circle. Your entire leg is moving with the same Angular Velocity, or else it would fall apart. But in order for this to be true, the tip of your leg has to be moving with a faster *Linear Velocity* than your knee. Thus, you will transfer more energy by hitting someone with the tip of your leg, and the longer your leg, the more energy you will be able to transfer.

Q: How does this apply to attacking with a weapon?
A: You will be able to transfer more energy by hitting with the tip of a weapon or with a longer sword or staff.

So where does the quantity of Force come in? Force is more of a steady state quantity, thus it is of more use to us in grappling. There are two key concepts we need to learn about.

Have you ever seen someone lie on a bed of nails and not get hurt? Why do we slap the ground on our falling techniques? The answer to these questions lies in the concept of Pressure. Pressure is simply the Force applied divided by the Area over which that Force is applied.

- **Pressure [$Pa = N/m^2$]** = Pressure equals Force divided by Area.

Pressure is what really causes impact injuries. When being stabbed by a knife, the Area is extremely small (only the knife point that touches your skin) so the Pressure is large. When a person lies on a bed of nails, the total surface area is the sum of the area of each small nail point. Thus the total pressure is not large enough to cause the nails to puncture the skin. When we do the falling techniques, we lower the Pressure by increasing the Area in contact with the ground.

As Martial Artists, we should be able to both concentrate and dilute a force to cause more or less damage.

The next concept is called Torque. Torque is what causes rotation. Torque is extremely useful in trying to flip an opponent or in applying most joint locks. Torque is sometimes referred to as leverage, and it is the product of the magnitude of the Force and the distance away from the rotational point.
- **Torque [NM]** = Torque equals Force times Distance.

For instance, say you are applying a joint lock on the thumb. Say you press at the near side of the thumb nail, 1 cm from the joint. Then say you instead press at the far end of the thumb nail, 2 cm from the joint. By only moving one centimeter away, you have effectively *doubled* the Torque on the joint and doubled the pain of your opponent.

The best way to cause rotation is to apply two forces such that they add together and both put Torque around the part of the body you want to rotate. Two forces acting in opposite directions is called a **Couple**. This is extremely important when trying to trip or sweep an opponent. Try to 'sweep' someone by putting your leg behind their leg and pushing on their shoulder, and then try the same thing while sweeping with your leg and pushing on their shoulder at the same time. Also, the farther both forces are from the point about which you are rotating, the larger the Torque. This is why can sometimes be easier to trip tall people, or why you are more stable in grappling when you spread out to a low and wide base.

This talk of tripping leads us to the next important concept, Balance. In order to be balanced, the integral (sum) of all the forces acting on your body must resolve to a vector that passes through some point on your body that is on the ground. Sound complicated? It's not. It merely says that if you lean one part of your body in a certain direction, in order to not be stable, you must lean another equal part in the opposite direction. Thus, when doing a side kick, your chest leans back while your foot protrudes outwards. When doing a spin hook kick, your chest leans down and away from the kick to counterbalance your leg.

Angular Momentum and Spinning Kicks

Angular Momentum (the tendency for something to keep spinning) is an important concept for spinning kicks. Angular Momentum is also conserved as long as no forces act on the system. This means that your rate of rotation multiplied by your moment of inertia about the axis which you are spinning will be constant. Or, in another way your shape determines how fast you spin.

The moment of inertia is the integral of each part of your body times the distance away from the axis you are spinning on. So, the farther your body parts are from your rotation axis, the larger your moment of inertia, and the slower you will spin. You've all seen ice skaters who start with their arms out (high moment of inertia) and then slowly move their arms in (low moment of inertia). What happens? They start spinning faster.

How can we apply these concepts to Taekwondo? Well, remember the importance of acceleration. Thus, you can change your speed quickly by starting with your arms and legs far out and then once you start a spin you can tuck them in quickly to get an extra boost. For instance, from open stance say you throw a butterfly kick with your legs and arms out. Your opponent will think that they have time to counter with their back leg roundhouse kick. But, at the last moment you bring your arms and legs close to your center and with the extra spinning velocity launch a back kick right into the unsuspecting player's stomach.

This concept is critical for doing advanced demo kicks like 540s and 720s. If you start the kick with your arms wide or legs spread, you can 'store up' extra spinning power that you will be able to call upon at the apex of your jump.

These concepts might seem difficult, but if you take the time to study them you will see that it is merely a more thorough way of describing things that you already know. As you go through high school and college, you will encounter these concepts again and by studying them now, you will have an advantage when you have to learn them later.

We have merely scratched the surface in terms of the technical analysis. There is much more to learn and discover. Fortunately, the KAT is at the forefront of the blending of science with martial arts. You will have a chance to help discover the physical principles behind martial arts techniques and help apply them to growing ourselves and our art.

The Importance of Quantifying Results

It's difficult to overstress how important it is to quantify your training results. That means that you **must** attach specific numbers to your outcomes if you want to get better as quickly as possible. It's much better to say "I stretched 165° today" rather than "I stretched far today." That way, you know what to shoot for the next day. You also know that if your max was 165, you shouldn't go for more than 170 the next day or you are likely to get injured.

Some things are difficult to quantify. You can still find a way around it. Instead of timing how long it takes you to do one roundhouse kick (which is hard to measure) measure the time it takes you to do ten roundhouse kicks, or twenty. Or, use a video camera and computer to analyze the number of frames from start to finish. Measure the height of your kick. Put a piece of tape on the floor and measure the reach of your roundhouse kick. You can even measure the number of steps or the time it takes you doing steps before you become too tired to do any more.

Measurement can also help you to predict your future performance, although this must be done with caution. Plot the performance on the Y axis and the amount of time you have been training on the X axis, and then pick an appropriate regression equation.

Measuring your technique also gives you the chance to evaluate different methods of training. One way of stretching might open your splits on average 3 degrees per week, while another might open them 5 degrees per week. Without measuring, you would only know that both ways make you more flexible. Think of it this way— if one way of training made you win all your matches and another way made you lose all your matches, which way would you train? Why shouldn't you apply the same reasoning to less complicated goals like doing the splits or having a fast roundhouse kick?

In order to learn more, we must increase the efficiency of our training.

So there are four important reasons to measure your technique.

- Know how far to push yourself
- Know when to stop to avoid injury
- Be able to determine which training method works better
- Predict future results.

Testing Requirements

Tae Geuk Yook Jang

"**Gam Gwe**" Water. Flow, endure obstacles with patience.

1. Left long stance, low block.
2. Front snap kick, left back stance turning middle block
3. Right long stance, low block
4. Front snap kick, right back stance turning middle block
5. Left long stance, right knifehand turning middle block.
6. Roundhouse kick, step down, left long stance, left turning high block, right punch.
7. Front snap kick, right long stance, left punch.
8. Right long stance right turning high block, left punch.
9. Front snap kick, left long stance, right punch.
10. Relaxed stance, low x block. (**5 Seconds**)
11. Right long stance, left knifehand turning middle block.

12.	Left roundhouse kick (*kihap*) step down right long stance low block.
13.	Front snap kick, right back stance turning middle block.
14.	Left long stance low block
15.	Front snap kick, left back stance turning middle block.
16.	Left back stance, middle knifehand guarding block
17.	Right back stance, middle knifehand guarding block.
18.	Left long stance, left push block, right punch.
19.	Right long stance, right push block, left punch.

Form 6 Key Points
•	The X block (move 10) should take 5 seconds.
•	Make sure to time the back stance turning middle blocks correctly on the first and third lines.
•	Step backwards with the right foot on the last move, and there is no *kihap* at the end of the form.

High Blue Belt Grappling Techniques
3.	**Clinch attack.** From the clinch, Bob gets one underhook and then does DUCK UNDER TAKEDOWN and gets the back. Alex rolls until he is facing upwards. Bob puts in hooks and applies CLOCK CHOKE. Alex removes one hook and turns over into Bob's guard. When Alex tries to pass Bob applies TRIANGLE CHOKE.

4.	**Defense against Takedown.** Alex shoots and then Bob defends by SPRAWLING. Bob uses CROSS FACE and BACK RIDE to get to the back. Bob applies BACK CHOKE and then ARM BAR from the back

Back Choke – The back choke is sometimes called the "kill the lion" choke. It is an arterial choke that lets you wrap around their neck and the real power comes from grabbing your own shoulder or arm and pushing down with your other hand.

Back Choke

Guillotine Choke – This choke works well from the guard or the person's back. This is a windpipe choke that goes straight across a person's neck.

Triangle Choke – The triangle choke is a very powerful attack that can often be launched when someone is trying to pass your guard. You wrap your legs around their head and trap one arm inside so that they have a very difficult time to break it.

Triangle Choke

Clock Choke – The clock choke is applied from the back mount. It was developed to be applied with an open gi but can be applied on a v neck dobak, sweatshirt, or even a t-shirt. It cannot be applied if your partner is not wearing a top. It is a carotid choke where one hand pulls one side of his uniform down at 6 o'clock and the other side over at 3 o'clock.

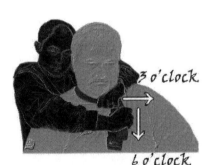

3 o'clock

6 o'clock

Clock Choke

High Blue Belt One Steps

10 (Red Stripe)	Step in with left leg long stance X block, turn and grab with right hand, double twist, left elbow to spine, left knee strike to spine, left hand groin pull from the back.
11 (Red Stripe)	Left outside to inside crescent, right spin hook, left butterfly to face and step through. End with left leg in front.
12 (Red Stripe)	Jump to right side with right foot and left front kick to groin, right jump front kick to face.

Korean Terminology Group 7: Stances (High Blue Belt)

Back Stance (*Deui Koop Yi*)	Front Stance (*Ap Koop Yi*)	Horse Stance (*Ju Choom Suh Gi*)	Walking Stance (*Ap Suh Gi*)
Tiger Stance (*Bum Suh Gi*)	Crane Stance (*Hakkdari Sugi*)	Cross Stance (*Dwiikeo Sugi*)	

High Blue to Red Belt Written Test

Congratulations! Don't forget to take pictures at the belt ceremony!

Name:
Date:
Board Break: Spin Hook Kick

What are your strongest and weakest points in Taekwondo sparring?

What are your strongest and weakest points in grappling?

How would you defend yourself against someone who is good at Muy Thai? How about Judo? Boxing?

How do you see your role in the school or club changing with your new red belt?

How do you say, 'Back Stance' in Korean?

There are a lot of equations related to Physics in this chapter. Choose one and explain it in terms of how it applies to your favorite technique.

High Blue to Red Belt Essay

Word of the Month:_____

Red Belt 3rd *Gup*

Red Belt Key Points

• You will keep red on your belt for longer than any previous belt since there are 3 red belt ranks and each one takes longer.

• Make sure you are giving back and helping others so you have something to write about on the black belt essays.

• It's very easy to get overwhelmed by the number of previous requirements if you don't keep up on them.

Lesson: Deceptive Motions (Faking)

Making deceptive motions is a very important part of Sport Taekwondo. In the black belt division, everyone has good technique. Everyone can kick hard and make a good strategy. How good they are at deceiving their opponent is one thing that separates the truly superior athletes. It is important to note that making deceptive motions should not be considered dishonorable, as long as it is within the rules. In fact, the ability to fool another skilled player is the mark of a great competitor. All deceptive motions have a few things in common. First of all, if you are faking a move, then your fake has to look like the beginning part of that move. The other thing to remember is that often a split second can make all the difference between success and failure. Thus if your fake can cause your partner to hesitate even that much, your attack will have a much higher chance of success. There are many types of deceptive motions that you may make in a match:

Fake an attack to draw out a counter – If your partner favors a certain counter attack, fake the related attack so that they can counter and then recounter their kick.

Fake a speed – Move at a slow speed for a few seconds so that your partner is lulled by your slower speed and then explode at a fast speed. Conversely, move very fast and then suddenly go slow. You may be able to catch them off rhythm.

Fake a direction – Get your partner to think you are moving one way and then switch quickly to take advantage.

Fake a mistake – Pretend to look at the scoreboard, slip, or be distracted. Then when he tries to attack you, have your counter ready.

Fake being faked out – It sounds a bit complicated, but when they do a fake, pretend that you fell for it, while being ready to recounter their counter.

Fake a strategy – The most common time this occurs is when you want to counterattack, for instance if you are winning and the time is running down. If your partner knows that he doesn't have to worry about your attack, his own attack will be more successful. Thus, keep making aggressive attacking motions and do one or two attacks to keep your partner's mind thinking of many things at once.

Check – This is not so much a fake, but you will stomp hard on the floor with your front leg while moving your body forward as if attacking. Checks can sometimes show you what your opponent was planning to do by how they move their body. It's a good idea to use checks before you attack because at the very least you can disrupt your opponent's rhythm.

Deceptive Telegraphing – This is an advanced technique where you can drop subtle hints to show you partner what you are planning to do. However, you show him things that you are not planning to do with the intention of leading him into a trap.

Lesson: Free Grappling

Free grappling is one of the most enjoyable parts of training for many students. Here are some pointers:

Grappling Rules

Some students are uncomfortable with certain grappling positions because they invade personal space. We try to respect this by in general not mixing genders when doing grappling techniques. However, if females wish to push themselves by grappling with males and there are no suitable female partners, then they will be allowed to at Sabumnim's discretion.

Although grappling techniques can be uncomfortable at first, it is important to get used to them. In an actual physical confrontation, the attacker often has the added advantage of you being uncomfortable on the ground. It is important to not give the attacker any added advantages. If you are more comfortable on the ground than him, you will be able to use this to your advantage and surprise him.

The most important rule is to know when to tap and when to release your partner. Taping the ground or your body is a way to signal to your partner that you have lost and wish to give up. If you cannot tap, you may say "TAP!" Either way, make sure that you are clear and loud so that your partner can hear you. If you are applying a lock or choke, you should anticipate your partner's tap. Children should tap once they begin to feel pain, while adults who are more experienced may tap once they know that they cannot escape from a lock. You must let go **immediately** upon a tap from your partner.

Grappling tips

In many ways, grappling is the opposite of sparring. While in sparring it is important to get to the target first, in grappling it is all about positioning. Speed can still be important, however. Yet, it is more important to be methodical. In grappling, you need to know first of all which position you are in, and how that position could either deteriorate to a less favorable position for you or improve into a more favorable position. Often, the position of one leg or arm can make all the difference between a very dangerous situation and one that is not so bad. Since grappling does not have breaks and we are training for real world self defense situations, endurance is more important here than in sparring. Thus, it is key not to waste energy. In sparring, you should appear to always be busy to avoid penalties. In grappling if something is not working, do not stick with it.

Here there is also the importance of thinking ahead. When someone is going for an arm bar and places their bottom leg around the far side of your head, perhaps they are setting up a triangle choke. Similarly, in order to attack someone's arm, you may have to bother their neck or cover their nose and mouth in order to force them to commit. These strategies are what separate a decent grappler from a beginning grappler. This is referred to as chaining. The key here is that when you try plan A, the defense your opponent tries may defend your plan A but open him up to your plan B. By switching quickly, you can always be one step ahead of him. See Grappling Drill 11 for a great example of this.

Be cognizant of your weight and how it is distributed. This will protect you against being reversed. You always want to keep a good base and the lower you are to the ground, the harder it will be to reverse you.

Point System of Grappling Matches

Most of our adult matches that we do in the *dojang* will go until submission. However, many grappling tournaments have a time limit and the winner of the match is determined by the score of points. Also, grappling for points can be appropriate for children and those who do not know submissions. The following point system is generally used:

Takedown from Standing (3 Points) – Takedown into a control position. A takedown to your opponent's guard is not a scoring technique.

Takedown from Kneeling (2 Points)

Guard Pass (3 Points) – Usually requires a control position to be held for at least 3 seconds.

Sweep (2 Points) – Going from guard to mount will get you points.

Mount (4 Points) – If you hold the mount for 4 seconds you will usually get 4 points. This is in addition to the sweep, takedown, or guard pass points you got to get there. For the back mount, you generally need to get your hooks in.

Lesson: Studying Opponents

It's important to understand how your opponents work, in order to find patterns in their attacks that you can take advantage of.

Psychology of Selection

Scientific studies show that reaction time increases based on the number of things that you are thinking about at one time.

For instance, imagine that you are sparring and you know that your partner is going to do one of two things (i.e., either attack the closed side or open side.) You have to mentally prepare a counter for both. If you wait to see what he is doing, then make a decision, then perform the counterattack, you have, say, a 50% chance of guessing correctly. However, if you have one counter in your head and prepare for it, and go for that one unless the other one comes, you may increase your chance of success. Say you have a 90% chance of a successful counter if you guess right, and a 40% chance if you guess wrong and have to adapt. Assuming that your partner has a 50% chance of throwing either technique, now you have a 65% chance of scoring.

In any case, the fewer things that you have to think about, the faster your reaction time will be. Thus, in sparring it's important to clear your mind and focus on just a few trains of thought. The more things that you can force your opponent to think about, the slower his reaction time will be.

Charles's Sparring Tips: (By Charles DeGuzman)

Charles DeGuzman is a third degree black belt and one of the KAT's top students. He was instrumental in developing advanced kicks and was one of the first people to do the 540 hook kick, winning the national championship in board breaking with it.

When sparring, it is important to know how to analyze your opponent, but before competition, you should already have various techniques to use in the ring. For instance, you cannot just step in there and use just one certain kick or footwork. Competition sparring techniques are grouped into three categories. There are the **circular kicks** (roundhouse and hook kick). These are called circular because they always hit the opponent from the side and require a good snapping motion. The second kind is the **linear kicks** (side, axe, push, and back kicks). They are linear because they always attack straight and most of the time rely on body weight rather than snap. Last are the **punches** (jab and reverse punches). These are rarely used for attacking. They are mostly used as a setup to open a gap between you and your opponent for your kicking attacks when countering. You have to have at least one kick from each kicking group, because they can easily counter each other. You should already know how to use punches. The more you know, the more you can confuse your opponent, but you can only go so far. Fancy techniques like 540 kicks or butterfly twist kicks will just cause you to lose points from easy counters or maybe put you in danger. Kicks are executed for their purpose at a certain time, not because they look pretty. You should also know which stances you need to use. Feet shoulder width apart gives you the quickest attacks. One and a half shoulder widths gives you some speed and some power. Two shoulder widths gives you the most powerful attacks. Stances vary with the situation. When you're far, you might use a wide stance for a powerful initial attack, but change to shoulder width fast stance when you get in almost to a clinch.

How do you study your opponent? Well, first you need to know little things like which foot is always forward, is he right or left footed, does he fight offensively or defensively, how long are his legs compared to yours, does he keep his hands down, does he like to be in an open or closed stance position, what's his favorite kick, what his reaction when you fake. Little things like these can help you a lot in choosing the right strategies. You can take advantage of his mistakes or counter his strategies. The second step is more technical. What happens when I do this or that kick from a certain position such as open or closed, or even from a clinch? Taking risks will help you to study your opponent, but you should always be aware of the consequences.

So what happens after that? Now that you know bits and pieces about your opponent, you can now apply them together with your techniques and use them against him. For instance, if he reacts to a round kick with a back kick, I would do a roundhouse motion feint and then counter that back kick. Here are some strategies to use against different types of competitors.

"He's Taller Than You." This will happen at least once in your sparring career. This means that he has longer legs than you in a sport that requires long legs. First of all, keep your hands up! A kick to your head could easily be just a kick to the torso for him. Second, you want to sidestep a lot. The longer the legs, the harder it would be for him to recover for a second attack after missing. Third, stay inside. When keeping in close, you cut off his attack and at the same time close your gap, causing him to retreat or jump back. It is a lot easier to attack forwards than back. Again keep your hands up. You are then in his high attack range. Fake and then move in. Make him throw a kick to miss you and then go.

"He's Shorter." It is pretty much the opposite of the tall strategy. You want to use a lot of cut kicks and fakes. The basic strategy is to keep your distance. When he comes in, cut him off with a linear kick (cutting sidekick works best), move to the side and attack. When you cut him off, he may not stop attacking. He may move out of the way and then attack with a roundhouse. When you side step, you're keeping the distance the way you need it to be for your counter. If you have enough speed, you can once in a while cut them off with an axe, back kick or a high roundhouse while jumping back.

"He's Too Aggressive." If your opponent loves to attack, let him for a while, but keep sidestepping or clinching. You can counter right after that sidestep and then clinch. Use the reverse punch to knock him off balance. Keep him wasting his energy and losing his points. Use a number of fakes to keep him paranoid and moving. One who kicks too much is often standing on just one leg. Knock him off balance with a linear kick and counter while he's attacking. Remember, the majority of points are from countering.

"He Waits A Lot and Counters." These types of sparrers are usually the smartest. The main thing you don't want to do is to attack aggressively with carelessness. Again, fakes are the main key. When they wait and counter, you want to make your fakes very convincing, because they know it's coming. When executing a feint, be ready for counters. Once he misses that counter, it's your turn. Use his own technique against him and clinch.

"This Guy's Fast." If your opponent is fast, you definitely don't want to have a speed contest. You will just end up being out-kicked. You want to attack when his leg is in the air. The time it takes to put his leg back down and attack a second time should be about the same or longer than when you throw your attack. You need to make him throw that kick to throw yours. How? Sidesteps and fakes.

"This Guy's a Heavyweight or Something!" That's your problem! You should have thought about losing weight before joining the competition.

A good sparer is fast, smart, can adapt to the situation and overcome his opponent; he must first learn to overcome himself physically and mentally, though. You should not be afraid to take risks in the ring. You must never be afraid to throw your kicks and attack. Always stay calm, relaxed, confident and in control. Everybody has great technique in elite competition. It is the mind that will separate first and second.

Video Analysis

Videotaping your sparring matches and technique is a very important part of your training. During a sparring match, things happen in a split second. Players and coaches are trained to read their opponents, but with all the adrenaline pumping and the limited time and vantage point, you are bound to miss something.

Studying tape is a great way to increase your skills. However, you must know what to tape and how to study it. At a minimum, you should tape all of your matches. If you can, you should also tape the matches of each person in your division. Even though you will not spar against all of them, you may spar them later. You will also get to see how they react in different situations. If you are not yet a black belt, then you should also try to take video of the black belt matches.

Now, what should you look for in your tapes? You will have to watch them many times over in order to see everything. First off, look for big lessons, i.e., things that are readily apparent. You will learn quite a bit about what techniques worked or didn't or major strategic errors or correct decisions you made. However, next you should look for details about your opponents and do statistical analysis on them. See if they prefer open stance or closed stance, and which leg they favor.

Fill out the following table by placing a tick mark every time the opponent does one of the following kicks.

	Attack Right	Attacked Left	Countered Right	Countered Left
Closed Stance				
Open Stance				

When you look at your own techniques, look for technical accuracy. This is often best done frame by frame in slow motion. If a technique failed, look to see why. For instance, did your back kick fail because you didn't react quickly enough, or was the path of your leg too wide? If the kick succeeded, note why it did so.

Next, note the deceptive movements that your opponents make and look for patterns. Do they always check one or two times before they strike? Do they always fake the open side before hitting the closed side? Or, do they always fake to the same place where they attack? Often, you will be able to notice patterns that your opponents themselves don't even know about. Knowing that, of course, you should do the same analysis on yourself, so that you don't fall into the same patterns. Of course, your opponent will not likely do the same thing *every* time, but if they do it 80 or 90% of the time, you can rely on it to get the jump on them in the next match.

Look for 'tells' in their techniques, i.e., small differences in how their fakes look and how their kicks look.

Also, look for things such as what their coach says or what motions he makes and what the player does. See how the player reacts when they are down on points, or see how they protect their lead. When there are only five seconds left and they need one kick to score, which kick does he attempt and how does he set it up?

You may even look at how people in the crowd react whenever you or your opponent scores a point. See what makes your opponent frustrated. If your opponent is difficult and you have not seen many people beat him, find someone who has and study how they did it. You may be able to use a similar strategy.

Testing Requirements

Tae Geuk Chil Jang

"**Gan Gwe**" Mountain. Stability and stop and moving with proper timing.

1. Left tiger stance, right hand push block.
2. Front snap kick, left tiger stance middle block.
3. Right tiger stance, left hand push block.
4. Front snap kick, right tiger stance middle block.
5. Left back stance, knifehand low guarding block.
6. Right back stance, knifehand low guarding block.
7. Left tiger stance, right push block with support, right back first to the face with support.
8. Right tiger stance, left push block with support, left back first to the face with support.
9. Attention stance, covered fist (*bojumok*) **(5 Seconds)**
10. Left long stance, scissors block and reverse scissors block.
11. Right long stance, scissors block and reverse scissors block.
12. Left long stance, forearm middle cross block.
13. Right knee strike, front cross stance double uppercut, step back to right long stance low forearm x block.
14. Right long stance, forearm middle cross block.

15. Left knee strike, front cross stance double uppercut, step back to left long stance low forearm x block.
16. Left walking stance, side backfist to the head.
17. Right out to in crescent kick, target strike, horse stance and middle target elbow strike.
18. Right walking stance, side backfist to head
19. Left out to in crescent kick, target strike, horse stance and middle target elbow strike.
20. Continue in horse stance, left middle knifehand block.
21. Step forward to right horse stance, middle punch, *kihap*.

Form 7 Key Points
- This form has a lot of details in terms of chambering and stances.
- Make sure to transition well between stances where both knees are bent and those where legs are straight.
- Know which hands go in the front for chambering.

Demonstration 5
1. Left long stance, right hand 45 degree downwards knifehand strike.
2. Right long stance, left hand 45 degree downwards knifehand strike.
3. Reverse long stance, left knifehand low block.
4. Reverse long stance, right knifehand low block.
5. Right back stance, stomp, right side backfist.
6. Right long stance, forearm scissors block. (Right hand middle, left hand low.)
7. Left back stance, stomp, left side backfist.
8. Left long stance, forearm scissors block (Left hand middle, right hand low)
9. Right front snap kick, turn, right tiger stance low knifehand cross block.
10. Left front snap kick, turn, left tiger stance low knifehand cross block.
11. Horse stance, left out to in middle block, right left double punch.

Grappling Drills 5 and 6

5. **Ground defense against striking.** Bob shoots and Alex defends by SPRAWLING. Alex uses HALF DUMP to get Bob in #2 position. Alex applies three knee strikes from #1 position. Bob defends and then SHRIMPS and puts in his guard. Alex tries to punch but Bob defends by pulling him close and then by applying FRONT CHOKE. Bob applies ARM BAR from the guard.

6. **Defense against headlock.** From Alex's headlock, Bob trips Alex backwards and kicks over take mount. When Alex tries to shrimp with hand on knee, Bob traps the arm at 90 degrees and rolls to his back to apply KIMURA LOCK and then OMAPLATA.

Front Choke – The front choke usually comes from the mount or guard positions. It's a blood choke where your knuckles dig into the sides of their neck. This choke works much better with a uniform or heavy coat on.

Omaplata

Omaplata – The omaplata is exactly the same submission as the Kimura lock, but it is applied with the legs instead of the arm. From the guard, when you go to the side, one of your partner's arms will be open to arm bar and the other one open to omaplata lock. Omaplata chains well with triangle. Make sure to prevent your partner from rolling by using your arm to stop him.

One Step Sparring:

13 (Red)	Left outside to inside knifehand block, spin arm and duck under to right tiger's mouth strike to neck.
14 (Red)	Step to right, left knifehand block, right punch to the jaw, go through and grab opponent's right shoulder, pull in and right knee to groin, pull head down, right back heel, guillotine choke.
15 (Red)	Step out to left long stance and right knifehand block. Trap opponent's arm and right roundhouse kick to stomach. Hook over and right hook kick to face followed by roundhouse kick to face. Spin, left spinning hook kick followed by left roundhouse to face.

Korean Terminology, Group 8: Kicks, Strikes and Blocks (Red Belt)

Kick (*Chagi*)	Block (*Maki*)	Punch (*Chi Roo Gi*)	Strike (*Chi Gi*)
Guarding (*Dae Bi*)	Knifehand (*Sohn Nal* or *Soo Do*)	Axe Kick (*Chicki Chagi*)	Back Kick (*Dwi Chagi*)
Crescent Kick (*Banh Dal Chagi*)	Flying Side Kick (*E Dan Yup Chagi*)	Front Kick (*Ap Chagi*)	Push Kick (*Meeroh Chagi*)
Side Kick (*Yup Chagi*)	Roundhouse Kick (*Dolyo Chagi*	Twist Kick (*Bee Teulo Chagi*)	

Red Belt to High Red Belt Written Test

You're almost there! Don't forget to take pictures at the belt ceremony!

Name: Date:

How are you going to fix your weak points before your black belt test?

What is torque and how does it apply to grappling?

A bridges B, passes B's guard, and then gets the mount. B shrimps out and then does a scissor sweep. What's the score?

Who was General Choi? What is important about his life?

What do you admire about the black belts in the school?

How have the people in your belt group helped you through difficult times?

Name two of your favorite kicks in Korean:

What are some strategies when sparring someone *taller* than you:

Red to High Red Belt Essay

Word of the Month:_____

High Red Belt 2nd *Gup*

High Red Belt Key Points

- You now have black on your belt, a color that will never leave!
- If you are old enough, start thinking about the possibility of having a career in martial arts.
- Start thinking about if you want to be a generalist or a specialist as a black belt.

Lesson: Fundamental Training Concepts

The above quote by my professor is one of my favorites, because it references a sentiment that is often subconsciously shared by students, namely that their progression should be relatively free from difficulty. However, this is not the case. If I went into a room full of ordinary people and asked "Who wants a black belt?" nearly everyone would raise their hands. However, if I asked who was willing to actually put in the work and time required, most hands would quickly drop. It is good that the world is this way, because otherwise you would not attach the same value to your accomplishments. One time after a hard practice when we were doing what seemed like endless situps, my instructor said *"Don't look at me. I didn't make this world. God is the one who made it so you have to push yourself through pain to get better."*

Whether or not you believe in God, there are several systems in the natural world that tend towards equilibrium and respond with stress when disturbed from that equilibrium. You can think of your progress as a 'spring' in the following general diagram. Different students have different 'stiffnesses' or spring constants, and progress at different rates.

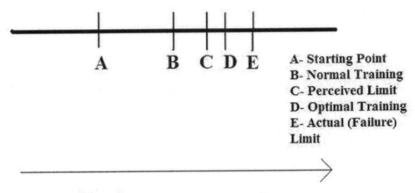

A- Starting Point
B- Normal Training
C- Perceived Limit
D- Optimal Training
E- Actual (Failure) Limit

A   B   C D E

Performance/Discomfort

The above picture illustrates some critical points with regards to training. Notice that the graph is only qualitative. A is where each martial artists starts, however, the starting points for various individuals can be at very different places. A 20 year old black belt will start each practice in a very different place from a 60 year old white belt. When we evaluate students, we take point A into account, and look only at the individual progress, not the absolute result. For the second person, doing twenty, solid pushups on a black belt test may be more of an accomplishment than the first person doing 100. During normal, self guided training, most people will progress to point B, somewhere below where they think their limit is. However, most people do not have a good idea how to gauge their actual failure limit. In order to reach the optimal training, an instructor must push the student to point D, somewhere beyond where the student thought that they could go (Point C). Most people place point C just after they begin to experience pain. Point E is the point where the student physically cannot go any farther.

For example, a student may come in and think that the most kicks that they could possibly ever imagine themselves doing is 1000 (C). After doing 800 (B), the student will think that they have gotten a great workout. However, in class with the support of the other students and the guidance of an instructor, they may be able to throw 1200 (D) kicks. They will be exhausted, but it is not until they throw 1500 (E) kicks that they physically cannot throw another kick. No matter their mental strength, their muscles simply do not respond.

When people work out, everyone has a set **'comfort zone'** (to the left of point C) and at the edge of this is a line where they think that their limit is. This is how you can tell someone who is experienced at martial arts, or competitive sports, or other kinds of discipline. They know where their limit actually is. As a student progresses, they should become more cognizant of these different points and where they lie at their current training level. Points C and E, the actual and perceived limits, should be much closer together on a black belt than in the general public. They should have an intuitive idea where the different points lie and how to progress most rapidly.

It is important to note that this graph represents one point in time. As the students travel along the graph, they pull the other points in the direction that they travel, with a force whose magnitude is proportional to the distance they are away from that point. For example, if a student often travels to point B, then his starting position, point A, will move to the right. If he frequently pushes himself to point C, then point A will again shift to the right, but this time it will shift farther and faster. If he goes to point D, then his starting position will shift even faster.

Unfortunately, the natural state of being is to be not good at Taekwondo. Thus, without practice, the student will drift slowly backwards. Thus there are two types of training, **maintenance** training, and **progressive** training. In maintenance training, the student puts in only enough work to counter the natural slip backwards. Maintenance training is useful for people who have already built up a solid base and are not actively competing for one reason or another. This can happen when a student goes off to college, goes through an extremely busy period in work or family life, on an extended vacation. It is the minimum training required to not lose ground. Progressive training is for the vast majority of students who want to actively get better. They must put in the training required for maintenance plus the training required to progress.

Point E, the absolute failure point, should be avoided, as point E is also the point where injury can occur. If injury occurs, then progress will be stopped and the student will naturally slide slowly backwards. See the next section for more information about types of pain.

Understanding where you lie and how to push your limits will help you to improve quickly. **A good instructor will never ask you to go past where your limit is, but he will ask you go past where you think your limit is.**

The Taekwondo relationship between a master and a student is very important. The student has to be willing to completely trust that the master is telling her what the best thing is, and the master has to know how to improve the student. A master's job for each student is to decide, using his experience, where the student's limit actually is. Then, their job is to push the student past where they think their limit is and closer to where they actually can go. They do this by yelling, joking, giving the energy of a group to feed off of, encouraging, etc. That's one of the things that makes a good instructor— the ability to get students closer to their actual limits.

Doing well in Taekwondo is not easy. If anyone tells you that it is, they are lying. Sure, many people do Taekwondo in a recreational way, where they come to class and work hard and enjoy it and then go home and return to their lives, and that is perfectly okay. There is something in Taekwondo for everyone, and people come here with all different ability levels. That said, many people who join Taekwondo want to become really good at it. And that is not easy.

Good Vs Bad Pain

When I say pain I'm going to mean all kinds of discomfort, primarily physical but also emotional. There are two different types of pain. There's the **'good' or 'natural' pain** and then there's the **'bad' kind of pain**. What's the difference? They both can hurt. The 'good' pain is the necessary kind of pain, and the bad pain is the

152

unnecessary kind. Now, what do I mean by necessary?

The way that the world works is that pain is often required for progress. Building muscles requires the buildup of lactic acid. Learning how to get hit requires getting hit. Learning how to hit requires hitting someone else. I think in general it's because progress requires being different form the 'resting state' You always need to inject energy to get away from equilibrium. We don't want to be average. That's not why we are training Taekwondo in the first place.

Once you can accept that this kind of pain is necessary, **pain itself loses its hold on you**. I can't stress this enough, because this is one of the major points. It's also one of the simplest, but one of the hardest for so many people to accept. For some reason now, there is this notion out there that life should be lived comfortably, without pain. This was never something that was expected in most societies throughout history. It seems to be a fairly recent invention. I would say even that living a life free of pain is somehow cheating yourself. You can't truly be happy unless you also know what it's like to be sad. Anyway, that's beside the point.

I said that Taekwondo is not easy, but also in general life is not easy. It's a trade off between difficulty and value. This is a problem in America today. Just look at the multi-billion dollar weight loss industry. Let me tell you— with few exceptions— loosing weight is easy. Well, the concept is— exercise more than you eat. It's just that simple. **If you burn more calories than you take in, you will lose weight**. Yet, we have extremely complicated and sometimes dangerous fad diets, fat and sugar substitutes, pills, creams, surgeries, metabolism boosters, etc.— this entire industry has been built up because people cannot accept the fact that they must work hard for things and do them the right way. If you look at the advertisements carefully, **all these 'magic remedies' are designed to somehow get around the basic relationship between eating less, exercising more and losing weight**. *"Eat what you want with this revolutionary new..." "Are you tired of fad diets, but exercise isn't for you? Then it's time you tried..." "Don't have time to spend with sweaty exercise? Well then..."* They all try to cheat the system and that's why none of them work. You must recognize that if you want something, you have to work to get it. This sounds simple but it's really profound in today's society, and this is why Taekwondo is all the more important. If you fail your black belt test, you have to keep working for it. If it were easy to become a black belt, then you wouldn't value it as much.

Sometimes the pain isn't as physical, it's more emotional. You have to work through these times, and they will clear. You'll get sad because you feel like you're not progressing as fast as you think you should, because one particular kick is not working, because you feel pressure to win, or because you keep losing. By putting in hard, pure work, you will be able to emerge from these times stronger than before.

Why don't students want to go past where they think that they can go to where they actually can go? It's because to go between those two points requires pain. It's as simple as that. People are afraid of pain, because on some level they can't accept the basic tradeoff. And, it's not an easy thing to accept. **But, once you do, you will see that pain will still hurt, but you will lose your fear of it.** In Taekwondo we're not interested in the feeling of pain, but only on how pain can affect performance. **Pain in and of itself should not affect performance.** It's only when one is afraid of pain, or unwilling to make the trade off, that pain becomes a detriment to progress, and something that the instructor has to work at to try to help the student push past. **If pain really does affect performance, that means either you're well past your actual limit (Point E) or that the pain is the bad kind, for instance from an injury.**

Now, this is all on an individual basis. Of course, we work out in a school. And, Taekwondo is hard. That's why only a small percentage of all the people that join ever become black belts. For many people, they can't accept this pain that is required for progress, and this is why they quit. But it's not only that. For other people, the pain might be fine, but they can't stand other people seeing them in pain. They don't want to show their vulnerabilities to their friends. But, once people do open up and share their pain with others, it makes them so much closer. That is one reason why the Taekwondo family is so close.

Now, the unnecessary or bad pain is pain that's outside of this normal tradeoff. This is the pain from injuries. Some people will want to keep working out when they're hurt. This is really bad, and **it ends up just making things worse in the end**. Say, if your knee is injured, but you keep kicking, you can injure yourself more and then you might not be able to work out for a long time. You could take off one month to heal, or work out that month and injure yourself more, forcing you to take off six months. The choice is obvious.

Progress Vs Time

Although each individual student progresses at a different rate depending on health, training, and other life factors, the general

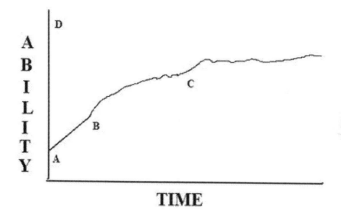

shape of student progress is shown in the following graph.

Note that the general shape of the graph could be described well by a logarithmic regression equation. There are several important things to notice. Point A is the starting point, often referred to as 'natural talent'. This could also be the result of previous training. The first phrase of training is the linear phase, between points A and B. This is the time in the beginning of training when the student sees direct results that are proportional to the training that they put in. In this stage, if the student trains twice as hard, he will progress twice as much. If he trains three times as much, he will progress three times as far. This is a great time for students as they see themselves progressing rapidly.

However, after point B, which occurs sometime around blue-red belt for most people, they start to see their progress taper off. Now, they may have to train three times as much to progress only twice as far. This can often cause a student to lose confidence in his abilities, as he is not seeing the same rate of progression that he did before. If a student is familiar with the fact that this is natural, he can use this knowledge to become less discouraged. Unfortunately, the farther along you progress, the slower your rate of improvement is. For advanced black belts, they may have to train ten times as much just to progress twice as far. In other words, the better you are, the harder it is to improve.

Point C seems to represent an anomaly in this graph, a time of rapid improvement. This can happen when a person sets his sights on getting better and puts all of his effort into improvement. He stops eating junk food, and starts eating only healthy food. He may start getting more sleep in order to be ready for the next day's training. This could include the period of time immediately leading up to a major tournament or black belt test.

Sometimes, a student may go through a period of improvement that doesn't seem to be directly related to an increase in training. This is usually due to a 'latent' increase that has been building up over a period of time, not unlike how when heating ice, the ice stays at 0° for a long time when heat is applied. That heat is used to break the bonds that are holding the water in its liquid state. In the same way, the training the student is undergoing is breaking the old habits and mental blocks down, and there is no measurable result on the outside.

Point D represents the student's potential, i.e., the highest level that that particular student can reach. It is often very difficult to know someone's true potential, and, sadly, most people will never reach it. Part of this is due to the inevitable fact that to reach one's ultimate potential, one must sometimes forgo other aspects of life, and this is usually not advisable or even healthy.

Whatever the case, knowing the shape of the training curve can help students avoid disappointment and better direct their energies to achieve the maximum results.

Lesson: Physiology of Training

It is important to understand the physiological effects of training on one's body, both on a general level and on an individual level in that everyone's body responds slightly differently to the types of training available to you. This section will briefly cover skeletal muscle and the cellular and molecular changes that happen during training.

Fatigue after an extensive workout is common; or even a light workout if you are not consistently training. Fatigue is the decreased efficiency and capacity of work that can be done by a muscle or the person as a whole. There are two types of fatigue that will be mentioned here. The first is psychological fatigue which is the most common type and usually the first that a person feels. Psychological fatigue is when a person perceives that any more work from the muscles is not possible. This corresponds to point C on the performance/discomfort graph. **This type of fatigue can be overcome!** Think of the last few seconds of a sparring match in a tournament. You are so tired that you can hardly bounce, but you are down by one point and then everybody starts to cheer you on… and then you feel yourself get excited and find the energy you didn't think that you had to throw one more fast kick to the head. That is an example of overcoming psychological fatigue.

The second type of fatigue is muscular fatigue, which is a physical fatigue that takes place in the muscle fibers. This is when there is too much ATP or energy depletion in the muscle and muscle contraction cannot function to full capacity. There is a physical decline in the tension that the muscle can produce. This fatigue is not perceived, but actual, and the muscles cannot be fully productive beyond this point. **Basically, this type of fatigue happens when your muscles have used up all the energy that they have, or have built up too many waste products to**

function efficiently. The stronger and better conditioned you are, the more that you can delay this type of fatigue. Although this is not an injury, this can be also thought of as the failure (absolute) limit represented by point E in the graph above.

What causes sore muscles? After extensive training, when muscles feel sore for the next day or two, it is due to the fact that slight damage has occurred to the muscle and the surrounding connective tissue during a workout with repetitive moves that quickly contract the muscles, such as kicking drills or even lunges where the muscles are stretched before handling a load. The pain that you feel is inflammation from the muscles in response to the microtears in the muscles and connective tissue. Being slightly sore is not a bad thing. In fact, it is the microtears that stimulate muscle growth. This is a healing process to build muscle, so it is not healthy to be training where you are sore every day. With consistent training your muscles should build to the point where you should not find yourself sore after most workouts, only those that are more extensive or active than usual, or those that focus on unique muscle groups that aren't used often.

Consistent exercise helps your muscles out in many more ways than just size and strength. There are two types of exercise: **aerobic, and anaerobic.** In Taekwondo, we use both types of exercise. We generally work from an aerobic base with anaerobic bursts. For instance, bouncing and moving around in a match is aerobic, but as soon as you go into a flurry and start kicking and kicking, your muscles are using oxygen faster than it can get to them which puts you in an anaerobic state. This aerobic/anaerobic mix is one of the things that make Taekwondo conditioning so difficult and unique. One good way to train is to go for a long jog, but alternate a minute or so of jogging with 15 seconds or so of sprinting. This will mix the two types of exercise in a way that you will need in a sparring match.

Aerobic Exercise - Aerobic exercise is when the body is working at a pace that oxygen delivery occurs at least as quickly as oxygen is being used in the cells for the production of energy. This is generally a decent cardio workout that is at a constant pace and doesn't leave you gasping for breath at the end of it. Aerobic exercise not only increases size, strength and endurance of muscles, it also increases the amount of nuclei, connective tissue, blood vessels and mitochondria that are associated with the muscles – increasing the potential overall performance of the muscles.

Anaerobic Exercise - Anaerobic exercise is basically when your body has used up your oxygenated energy, and now is producing the energy you need to continue through anaerobic respiration which is the production of energy in the absence of oxygen. This energy production is much more limited in duration than aerobic energy, but is a fast production of energy for sprinting or fast double kicks and has the metabolic byproduct of **lactic acid**. Lactic acid build up is responsible for the "knots" in your muscles, and is released from the muscle fibers into the blood stream. Lactic acid is also responsible for the soreness that you feel after a workout. Too much lactic acid in the blood stream can make you sick, so it is very important to drink a lot of water after any good workout and the day after to help move the lactic acid through your system.

Muscle relaxation is the opposite of contraction, yet it also requires energy. Energy is required in the transportation of specific elements within the muscle cells, and once these elements bind to a specific site, if the muscles need to contract again, more energy is needed than if the muscle hadn't relaxed in the first place. This is just to illustrate that it is not energy efficient to let muscles relax in the middle of say an hour long workout. It is best to let the muscles relax at the end of your use of them unless you plan to work out for half a day or more at one time. **These elements that are required are Calcium, Sodium, and Potassium. A lack of any of these can lead to difficulty contracting and relaxing muscles**. This is essentially what happens during a cramp. These elements are known as electrolytes, and are a major component of sports drinks.

Some people use anabolic steroids to increase the size and strength of their muscles. Anabolic steroids are related to and similar to testosterone in that they increase the size of muscles. However, studies have shown many severe side effects with the use of anabolic steroids including heart attacks, strokes, testicular atrophy, irritability, sterility and abnormal liver function. Of course, KAT students should never use them, as this represents going around the normal 'good pain' relationship.

A healthy body will support you best with a natural workout plan that will increase the limits of your body in parallel with awareness and a strong mental understanding of your capabilities.

Lesson: Psychological Effects of Training (by Liz Brewer)

Liz Brewer is a 2nd degree black belt with Auraria Campus Taekwondo and KAT. In 2006, she graduated with a degree in psychology from Metro State College of Denver. One of her major projects was the impact that training had on the self-esteem of the participants.

Self-esteem has been studied for many years over many different demographics. Age, gender, nationality, and socio-economic status can influence someone's self-image and therefore affect their self-esteem. Methods of increasing self-esteem often involve both physical and mental changes in a person's life. A healthy self-esteem is critical for healthy living. Martial Arts involve both the body and the mind and are a form of exercise that can increase a person's awareness and self-esteem. According to the United States Martial Arts Association, Martial Arts has been "proclaimed by many to be a great activity for both children and adults for building self-confidence and self-discipline."

A research project was conducted in 2005 at the Metropolitan State College of Denver to study the relationship between participating in martial arts and self-esteem. Taekwondo was used as the martial art for this research study, because of its increase in popularity in the college community as well as its growing recognition as an Olympic sport. Participants from both Level I and Level II Taekwondo volunteered to fill out the Coopersmith Self Esteem Inventory. Non-martial art students were also used as a baseline. **The results of the study show there is a positive correlation between participation of martial arts and self-esteem.** The positive correlation is that as participation in martial arts increases, so does self-esteem. The research also indicated a positive correlation for women and increase in self-esteem. The increase of participation in martial arts also has the benefit in increased overall personal health for participants.

Self-esteem is something that shapes who a person is and how their future decisions are made. It is common for someone with low self-esteem to make either poorer decisions or ones that are less thought out. When a person has more confidence in who they are, they trust their decision-making skills more and that is reflected in how others see them as well. Martial arts not only improve a person's health and overall physical appearance by getting them into better shape, but martial arts also improve a person's inner self as well. They become better people who respect themselves and others, because through martial arts they build a community worth doing good for. This is why it is more common for people who are in martial arts to do better academically, have higher self-esteem, and be better behaved.
Martial arts teaches both inner and outer strengths.

When someone has more self-respect and higher esteem, they act more positively towards others. This turns around in their favor, because more people will treat them with respect as well. That person will then see that they are respected and therefore maintain a high esteem for themselves. This can also be true in a negative way. **If a person thinks they are worthless, they will act like they are worthless.** This attitude will then affect those around them and how they are treated. When that person sees that they are being treated poorly, this will confirm their idea of being worthless. **A self-fulfilling prophecy can be a very powerful tool in shaping how someone sees their life and how others treat them. By harnessing this in a positive light, this can establish brighter futures and more productive outcomes, because ultimately self-esteem is the attitude that we bring to life.** This translates into 90% of communication, while only 10% is the actually talking that occurs.

In short, Taekwondo has been scientifically shown to make you healthier on the inside as well as the outside!

Lesson: Health and Injuries

Taekwondo has been shown to be extremely beneficial to the health of its participants. In general people who practice Taekwondo will lose unhealthy weight, become more alert and focused, and build strength in their muscles and joints.

However, as with any contact sport, there will be injuries, mainly bumps, bruises and strained muscles, but sometimes more serious injuries will occur. Taekwondo is a great immune booster— people who practice Taekwondo vigorously are very rarely sick. Still, there will be times when every student is ill. It is important to treat these illnesses and injuries properly so that there will be a minimum disruption in training.

The best way to deal with injuries and illnesses is to prevent them in the first place. Here are some keys to preventing injuries and illnesses before they occur:

- Always warm up and stretch before undergoing strenuous exercise. We will warm up in class but you should arrive a few minutes early to stretch out and warm up any body parts that might require extra care.
- Wrap or tape body parts that might require extra support. This will also serve to help keep them warm.
- Bring a warmup jacket to wear after practice, even during the warmer months. Sudden changes in body temperature caused by the sweat on your body can be shock to your system and lead to reduced immune system performance.
- Be cognizant of the fact that especially during sparring competitions, you will have a large amount of adrenaline. So, an injury may not seem as bad as it actually is.

The P.R.I.C.E. acronym is easy to remember and helpful for dealing with injuries when they occur.

P- PAUSE The most important thing when you get an injury is to STOP what you are doing. Even if the pain is less because of adrenaline, further exercising could cause much more serious damage.

R- REST For most injuries, rest is the most important thing you can do. Better to rest one week than work out and injure it further, making you sit out for one month. Rest need not be total. For instance, with a sprained ankle, you might still be able to do a bench press, or still do forms with a broken hand.

I- ICE Ice causes the blood vessels around the affected area to dilate (open up) and let more blood through in order to heat the area back up. This is why your face gets red when it is cold out. More blood going to the area brings healing factors and flushes out damaged tissue. Ice should be covered with a towel and kept on for 10-15 minutes.

C- COMPRESSION Compression of the affected area helps reduce swelling, which can reduce performance and cause pain and discomfort. Compression can be achieved with an ace bandage.

E- ELEVATION Lifting the affected body part above the level of the heart will use the force of gravity to help reduce swelling. This can be done by propping an affected ankle on some pillows or sitting on the floor and putting an affected arm on a chair.

The following is from a computer simulation performed by Master

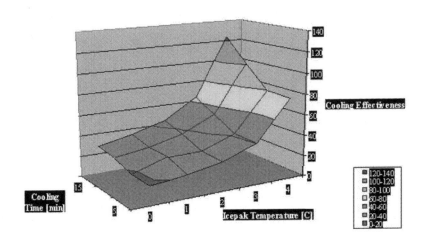

Bill Pottle and Sherry Lai and Jeff Lee (both second degree black belts) on what happens when ice is applied to a bruised area.

This graph shows the 'cooling effectiveness' a figure that takes into account the penetration of cooling and the potential for tissue damage. As you can see it is better to apply a slightly higher temperature ice pack (or wrap it in a towel) for a longer time.

Lesson: Nutrition

"There are only two times you need to worry about drinking water—when you're thirsty and when you aren't." – Boy Scout Proverb

Everyone knows that proper nutrition is the key to good performance. You wouldn't fill a race car with crude oil and expect it to win a race. Your body is the most complicated and intricate machine on the face of the earth. You can't fill it with junk and expect it to perform well. In computer science this is called GIGO – Garbage In, Garbage Out.

Still, what specific foods should you eat or not eat? That depends on what your long and short term goals are. In general, everyone should eat a balanced diet that includes grains, milk and cheeses, meat and protein sources, fruits and vegetables, and a small amount of sugars, oils, and fats. It is important to make sure you get enough trace vitamins and minerals, especially the B vitamins. If you are worried that you aren't getting enough vitamins, you can take a supplement, although this is not needed for most people. Many students come to Taekwondo with the intention of losing weight. In this case, it is wise to limit intake of complex carbohydrates and grains. Many other students want to gain weight and muscle, and in this case you must consume large amounts of protein.

You can occasionally eat candy and drink soft drinks, but these should be used sparingly as they have little or no nutritional value and will only end up adding fat weight. Sports drinks are good to drink after practice to replace lost minerals, but some students will want to dilute them with water during competition as their body may not be able to handle the high electrolyte content.

Water is extremely important. Not only is it a critical component in countless biological processes, hydration is critical for maintaining a sharp mind, flushing out metabolic wastes, and balancing electrolyte concentrations. You should drink large amounts of water both before and after practice.

Lesson: Cutting Weight

There is a clear advantage to being taller than one's opponent. Since Taekwondo tournaments divide the competitors according to weight divisions, having a large height/weight ratio is advantageous. Since little can be done to affect height, most competitors will try to drop their weight to get into a lower division.

While cutting weight is not wrong, it can be dangerous if done in an unsafe way. People go through natural weight fluctuations with the time of day and the amount of food in their stomachs. Before deciding to cut more than five pounds, you must get Sabumnim's permission. At that time we will work together to develop a safe and effective plan for lowering weight before the weigh in. There is not only a danger that you may become physically unhealthy, but there is also the danger that your performance will suffer more than if you had stayed in a higher division.

Here are some tips for cutting weight:

- Try to weigh in in the morning before you have had anything to eat or drink.
- Eating salty foods will cause you to retain water and make it difficult to lose weight.
- Always weigh yourself at the same time and in the same attire
- Zero the scale periodically to make sure it is accurate.
- Get down to your appropriate weight at least 3 days prior to the competition to get used to the new weight.
- Immediately drink water after weighing in.
- Make sure to take multivitamin supplements when restricting your diet.

Testing Requirements

Grappling Drills:

7. **Throw from clinch.** From the clinch, Bob takes down Alex with HEADLOCK THROW. Bob applies SIDE CHOKE, then kicks over to ARM BAR FROM #1 POSITION

8. **Leg Submissions**. From Alex's guard, Bob breaks the guard and goes for ANKLE LOCK, but Alex grabs the head and sits up to take the mount. Bob bridges and returns to Alex's guard and breaks it again, this time going for KNEE BAR. Bob lets go and then transitions to KNEE LOCK and finally takes Alex's back.

Form 8 Tae *Geuk* Pal Jang

"**Gon Gwe**" Earth. Embrace other students as the earth embraces life

1. Step forward to left back stance, guarding block.
2. Step out left long stance, right middle punch.
3. Jump double front snap kick (right-left), *kihap*, left long stance out to in middle block, right-left double punch.
4. Right long stance middle punch.
5. Reverse long stance, half mountain block.
6. Left long stance, hair pull, slow uppercut (**8 seconds**)
7. Step in front, reverse long stance, half mountain block.
8. Right long stance, hair pull, left slow uppercut (**8 seconds**)
9. Left back stance, knifehand guarding block.
10. Step out to left long stance, right middle punch.
11. Front snap kick, step step back to right tiger stance, push block
12. Left tiger stance, knifehand guarding block.
13. Left front snap kick, left long stance right hand punch, come back to left tiger stance push block.
14. Right tiger stance, knifehand guarding block.
15. Right front snap kick, right long stance left hand punch, come back to right tiger stance push block.

16. Right back stance, low forearm guarding block.
17. Left front snap kick, pause, right jump front snap kick, *kihap*, right long stance, out to in middle block, left – right double punch.
18. Left back stance, left knifehand middle block.
19. Left long stance, right elbow, right backfist, left punch.
20. Right back stance, right knifehand middle block.
21. Right long stance, left elbow, left backfist, left punch.

Form 8 Key Points

- This form has the opposite pattern of form 1, going from the third line to the second and then to the first.
- It's difficult to begin and end in the same spot.
- Know the difference between both types of jumping kicks.

One Step Sparring

16 (Black Stripe)	Right inside to outside crescent, left step on knee, check off and right spin hook to face.
17 (Black Stripe)	Step in right back stance knifehand middle block, slide in and right knifehand strike to temple, scissors takedown, left knifehand to neck on ground
18 (Black Stripe)	Step out with the left foot long stance and right knifehand block to receive punch, pull opponent and spin, reverse direction, step over, arm bar, let opponent come up into your triangle, and then continue to omaplata.

Korean Terminology - Group 9: Body Parts and Directions (High Red Belt)

Down (*A Rae*)	Backward (*Hoo Jin*)	Forward (*Chun Jin*)	High Section (*San Dan*)
Low Section (*Ha Dan*)	Middle Section (*Choong Dan*)	Side (*Yup*)	Front (*Ap*)
Ball of Foot (*Bal Ba Dak*)	Body (*Mom Tong*)	Face (*Ul Gool*)	Foot (*Bal*)
Foot Edge (*Bal Nal*)	Head (*Muh Rhee*)	Heel (*Bal Deui Geum Chi*)	Inside (*Ahn*)
Instep (*Bal Deung*)	Knee (*Moo Reub*)	Neck (*Mok*)	Outside (*Bak Got*)
Posture (*Ja Se*)	Waist (*Huh Rhee*)	Wrist (*Pal Mok*)	Pressure Point (*Koop So*)
Right (*Oh Reun*)	Left (*Wen*)		

High Red to Double Stripe Red Belt Test

The last test before your black belt test. Don't forget to take pictures at the belt ceremony!

Name: Date:

Board Break: Any Hand Technique

Describe black belt tests that you have seen before.

What do you want your test to be like?

Who is in your belt group now? Are you going to test for black belt together?

Explain the story of Admiral Yi Sun Shin. Research online. Your new form is named after him.

What is the difference between 'Good Pain' and 'Bad Pain'?

Fill in the Acronym, PRICE for dealing with injuries:

P:

R:

I:

C:

E:

Instead of the essay this time, submit your weekly workout schedule.

Weekly Workout Schedule

Make a training plan for every week. 10-15 hrs minimum is a good amount before the test. Be specific in your notes.

Day	Requirements	Conditioning	Free	Other
Monday				
Tuesday				
Wednesday				
Thursday				
Friday				
Saturday				
Sunday				

Double Black Stripe 1st *Gup*

Double Black Stripe Key Points

- This is it- the period right before your black belt test should be one of the most memorable in your life. Don't short change yourself.
- A black belt is like a pilot's license – sure, it is a cool accomplishment on its own. But the real beauty comes when you use it.
- Submit the proposed workout log after the test.

Black Belt Procedures

A school is judged by the quality of its black belts.

After you receive your First *Gup* belt you'll embark on the **black belt test preparation period**, a time when you'll push your limits in all areas of your life. The black belt test is by far the most difficult test, and the test where most students are asked to retest or put off their testing. You don't have to be perfect. In fact, a 1st degree black belt is roughly equal to a high school diploma.

One of the worst things that can happen to a martial arts student is receiving a black belt that they didn't earn.

The training until first *Dan* is very general, while for higher Dans students should choose an area of training to specialize in.

Black Belt Certification- All KAT black belts are certified through Kukkiwon (World Taekwondo Federation Headquarters) in Korea. This process takes several months to complete. However, the certificate is recognized throughout the world.

KAT black belts are also separately certified through KAT. This certificate recognizes things that are part of the test that are above and beyond what is required on the Kukkiwon test, including grappling, one step sparring, multiple opponent sparring, community service, etc.

Three classes of requirements.
- **Technical Skills**– Know everything on the requirements board inside and out. Period.

- **Applied Skills**- Use your knowledge in free sparring, free grappling, and board breaking. Show strength, adaptability, strategy, ability to read partners, etc.

- **Nonphysical Skills** – Show leadership, mental understanding of the history and philosophy of Taekwondo, and maturity to know when to use what you've been taught.

Performance Based vs Effort Based- Except for very special circumstances, the testing is only performance based. That means you cannot pass the test simply by trying hard. Effort will be considered, but the performance must be there.

Black Belt Training Period- In many ways, the training period is more important than the test itself because this is the time when you must work harder than ever before to overcome all of your challenges and deficiencies. This time should change your life.

6 Months before the test (May be 3 months before for actively training students going for 2nd + *Dan*)
- Submit workout log to Master Bill (Schedule both inside and outside of class on how you are going to get ready) ~ 15 hours/week minimum.
- Begin stepping up all training
- Begin working on essay questions (Available in Electronic form)
- Begin planning for Leadership Service Project

Leadership Service Project
- This is a time for the student to demonstrate his ability to lead others and focus his efforts on a worthwhile goal.
- The project need not be large, but should be chosen, organized, funded, carried out, and reported on by the student.
- The student must enlist the help of at least 10 other people to carry the project out.
- A report with pictures should be included in the application

Sample Black Belt Service Projects

The key is to pick something that you are passionate about. Make the world a better place! Get at least 10 people to help you, and raise any needed $ yourself.

Make a Video – Make a video promoting self-defense, bully awareness, environmental or health issues, etc. Get friends to be in it, write the script, and then give out DVDs and post to YouTube.

Trial Maintenance – Pick a section of trial in the mountains and do work preventing erosion, clearing overgrowth, etc.

Safety Survey – Go through your neighborhood asking about common safety hazards (ie, smoke detectors, Carbon Monoxide detectors, etc.) and offering to help fix issues. Work with the fire department.

Minor Construction Projects – Visit a soup kitchen, homeless shelter, etc. and ask if they need anything built. Master Bill built 3 sets of food shelves for his Eagle Scout project for St. Andrews Shelter- previously they had to let the donated food sit on the floor.

Food/Blankets/Clothing Drive – Get your friends to go out and place boxes in several areas. Collect the items and donate to a worthy charity. Consider shipping to a foreign country or US soldiers abroad. You can also do things like get used glasses and give them to Lens Crafters.

Soldier Appreciation – Get all the students together to make some cards/care packages for US Troops stationed abroad or veterans here at home.

Tree Planting – Get some trees together and plant them in the forest or land here in town. Perhaps plant a free tree in each student's house if they wish.

Registration Drive – Register for people to vote, get library cards, or especially join something like a bone marrow registry. This project could save lives.

Church/Mosque – Many churches or other religious places have projects that need doing. Ask and see what you can do.

Emergency Preparedness – Make emergency kits (radios, water pur, etc) and teach others to do the same. Keep the items in your house in case of disaster.

Self Defense Seminar – Give a seminar to your school, etc. Ron Roe taught falling technique to a group of head injury survivors. Or start a team at your school.

For more ideas see: http://www.scoutorama.com/project/

Competition Philosophy

Competition- an important part of our training, not our ultimate goal.

There has certainly been much debate over the proper place of competition in martial arts. The value of two competitors training "live" with each other, or sparring against a resisting opponent rather than just practicing forms should have been apparent to everyone since the decisive victory of Jigoro Kano's Kodokan Judo at the Tokyo police tournament of 1886. The Kodokan students practiced free sparring and the other schools practiced only forms.

The best thing about competition is that **competition always leads to innovation**. Just look at the success of capitalism over communism during the last century. Without competition, School A has technique A and School B has technique B, and both assert that their way is superior. With competition, the public can see which technique actually works better, and thus the martial art improves, with other schools free to build off the base. This is one reason for the rapid technological development of Taekwondo over the last 40 years. **Competition provides an important 'reality check.'** I know there have been times that I thought what I was doing was working, only to step into the ring and find out that my training wasn't enough. Competition also teaches us patience, how to deal with adrenaline, how to figure out an opponent quickly, how to perform even on your bad days, and builds team spirit. Thus, competition is an important *part* of our training.

However, this is really the key. The ultimate goal of our training is to become a better person and a better martial artist, not solely competition. This is what distinguishes Taekwondo from other sports. Competition should be seen as a *means* only, not an end in and of itself. Some schools think that the only purpose of their training is competition. This leads to three main problems. First, they may engage in behavior at the tournament that is not frowned on in other sports, but is very disrespectful for Taekwondo. No match is important enough for you to throw your helmet or cuss out the referee or hit your opponent with a cheap shot. Consider this your warning that that type of behavior will not be tolerated by KAT students. Secondly, this exclusive focus on competition may cause the school to neglect other important areas of training, such as self-defense. Thirdly, if competitions are seen as the most important thing, people will tend to have a mental lapse after a tournament is over, and only train hard once a tournament is coming up. You must train hard all the time, regardless of when the competition is. Training when others are resting is the only way to make up ground on people who are better than you, because before the tournament when everyone is training hard everyone is progressing.

The last thing I would like to mention about competition is the terminology. Although this is not strict, it is proper to refer to people sparring as competitors, athletes, or sparrers, rather than fighters. It is proper to refer to the match as a match, not a 'fight.' The reason for this is that a sparring match is very different from a real fight. Olympic Style sparring does not have much to do with fighting, thus it is not proper to say that someone who is a good sparrer is a good fighter. Many elite Taekwondo athletes could be taken down and choked out by someone with only an elementary knowledge of grappling.

The KAT has historically done very well in competition, and now it is time for us to step up our training even more. With the proper attitude, competition can go a long way towards making us better martial artists.

Competition Format

Taekwondo competition is conducted in tournaments hosted by an individual school (KAT Tournament) or by a league or national governing body (USA Taekwondo or AAU National Championships). The format of each tournament is determined by the host. However, most tournaments generally follow the same rules with little variation.

In general the tournament will have individual events of forms and sparring. Some tournaments may also have events of board breaking, creative or group forms, weapons forms, grappling, blaster pad sparring, or tag team sparring. For sparring, you will be placed into a single elimination bracket that branches out. Each level of the bracket represents one match that you have to win. The number or levels can be determined by the lowest integer value of n such that $2^n >=$ number of competitors. For example, if there are 15 players, then there will be 4 ($2^4 = 16$) rounds. Unless the number of competitors is a perfect power of two, some competitors will have a bye to the next round. In local tournaments the bye selection is usually random, in national tournaments they seed competitors based on their previous record. Bracketing is usually done to prevent competitors from the same school from meeting in the first round of the tournament. In most tournaments both the semifinal losers will be awarded third place. Thus the total number of matches to run a division is the number of competitors minus one. (One person must lose each match and each person but one must lose exactly once.) You can also see that doubling the number of competitors only increases the number of matches you must spar by one. Some tournaments may also have round robin or double elimination brackets. This information should be published ahead of time.

Sparring consists of two or three rounds of approximately two minutes each. Lower ranks and children will spar less, upper ranks and adults more. During those times one player wears a blue chest protector (*hogu*) while the other wears a red one. You try to score points by kicking and punching the other player while avoiding penalties. Matches are usually decided by who scores the most points, but in the adult (14+) black belt division matches can be decided by knockout as well. During the breaks you will get to rest and talk to your coach. If the match is tied and the judges are using electronic scoring, then the match will proceed to sudden death. Most matches are scored electronically, where if two judges press their score buttons within one second, then a point goes up for that player. One point is awarded for kicks and solid punches to the *hogu* and three points are awarded for kicks to the face or head. There is an additional point awarded for spinning techniques. For more information on sparring, see the chapter earlier in the book. Also, Taekwondo rules often change in a minor way every few years. See the websites of various organizations mentioned earlier for up-to-date rules.

It is important to remember that whatever happens in the tournament you must be a good sport. Of course we want to win every time, and we will practice hard to make it happen, but that is just not possible. Remember, you only truly lose a match if you do not learn anything from it. After the match, regardless of the outcome, you must shake hands with and congratulate the other player. You must also congratulate his or her coach. Even in sparring tournaments, respect and discipline are the most important things.

In forms competition, two people will perform their techniques and the judges will give a score from one to ten. If there are five judges then they will drop the low and high scores and add the middle three. The winner is the competitor with the highest score, and they often will not give two third places. The judges look for good technique, balance, beginning and ending in the same spot, strong yells, and good discipline. They are generally not as strict on the technical details of the form, as different schools may perform a form in slightly different ways. Sometimes they will have double elimination in forms competitions as well. There may also be a sport poomsae competition which would be a different event.

In breaking or weapons competitions, they usually score the same as in forms. Usually, the criteria for scoring are made available ahead of the tournament date so that the competitors will know what to do. Sometimes there are time or area limitations.

Lesson: Competition and Tournaments

Tournaments are one of the best times that you will share with your Taekwondo friends. These are the times where the team will unite and show the sacrifices that they have been making in practices. During these emotional times you will see yourself and your teammates rising to levels you never thought possible, and you will feel whole ranges of emotions from fear, to exhilaration, to pain, to joy, to being part of something larger than the sum of its parts, to being completely alone. But the most important thing about going to tournaments is making sure that everyone is safe. The biggest danger is not usually the tournament itself, but traveling there and back, sometimes late at night on bad roads. With a few simple tips however the tournaments can be a more enjoyable experience for everyone:

Note: Many of these tips apply to trips out of town with an overnight stay. Most of our tournaments are local.

Packing- Bring only your gear, dobok, belt, student ID card (if needed), sleeping bag, personal items, and any medicines or food you might need. Oftentimes, the cars or busses are crowded, and we are usually gone only a bit more than one day. If you use a particular medicine, (i.e., albuterol inhalers) know who else on the team uses the same thing just in case.

Food- Be sure to bring some extra food including juice, Gatorade, or a water bottle. Learn what food you can and can't eat before a match. It's also good to have extra food to eat after you are done.

Adrenaline- Your natural response to the impending competition will be to build up adrenaline in your blood. This will help you kick harder and think clearer during the tournament. You will also be numbed to pain and feel a euphoric feeling. You might have to use the bathroom a lot or feel nauseous. However, when the competition is over your adrenaline levels will subside quickly and you need to be careful to rest enough.

Cars- The ride home can be dangerous if we don't return home until late at night. People are tired, sore, and emotionally drained. If possible, it's better to have someone who didn't compete or competed only in forms drive. The car ride home can be the most dangerous time of the tournament. Whoever is not driving has the responsibility of keeping the driver awake. Talk about the tournament, about other tournaments, about your life story, play loud music, drink caffeine, do anything to keep the driver awake. The responsibility of the people in the back seat is to keep the people in the front seat awake. During these times is when we really bond, when, "it's a long story" isn't an excuse not to tell something anymore, when all the life stories come out. If worst comes to worst, pull off to a rest stop and sleep for a couple of hours before continuing on your way.

At the tournament- One of the reasons that tournaments are so hectic is that there are so many things that need to be done. Everyone, regardless of rank, needs to help out all day in order to get things done on time and done well. This is especially critical for any black belts that can help out refereeing and judging- **this is the one single factor that will make the tournament run faster.** There is something for everyone to do, however. Whether it's taping matches, holding pads, coaching, judging, timing matches, finding athletes who are lost, or just cheering as loudly as possible for KAT and ACT, we need to act as a team to win. Also, at the tournament be sure to watch other matches, especially your division or the black belts. This will help you tremendously to learn. Make sure you listen to your coaches. Depending on the tournament and how many students are competing, you might have one coach with you the whole time, or other coaches who help you warm up and another coach that just steps into the ring with you. Tell them if anything feels wrong. KAT Masters have been to hundreds of tournaments and are there to make sure you do your best and have a positive experience.

Testing Requirements

9. **Kick Defense.** Alex comes at Bob with a roundhouse kick, and Bob scoops under and does KICK DEFENSE TAKEDOWN. Alex holds Bob in the guard and goes for KIMURA LOCK, but Bob defends with REVERSE KIMURA LOCK. Bob then uses BEHIND THE BACK GUARD PASS to get to #1 position. From there, Alex tries to fend him off and Bob uses FAR SIDE ARM BAR.

10. **Wheel Throw Series.** Alex comes to push Bob and Bob counters with WHEEL THROW. Bob runs to put Alex in #4 position and applies KIMURA LOCK. Alex escapes by rolling backward to get the back mount. Alex tries to apply BACK CHOKE but Bob crosses Alex's legs and applies CROSSED ANKLE LOCK.

One Step Sparring

Create 3 of your own. It's pretty open-ended, but show good technique, good flow, good control, and be creative. This is your time to shine!

Board Break: Butterfly, Spinhook combo. Flying Side kick over your chosen obstacle(s).

Taeguek Il Jang (Moves in Korean)

1. *Ap sugi, palmok arae maki* (walking stance, forearm low block, etc.)
2. Ap sugi, jumok momtong jireugi
3. Ap sugi, palmok arae maki
4. Ap sugi, jumok momtong jireugi
5. Ap kubi, palmok arae mako, pandero jumok momtong jireugi
6. Ap sugi, pandero toylo momtong maki.
7. Ap sugi, pandero jumok momtong jireugi
8. Ap sugi, pandero toylo momtong maki.
9. Ap sugi, pandero jumok momtong jireugi
10. Ap kubi, palmok arae mako, pandero jumok momtong jireugi
11. Ap sugi, palmok ulgool maki
12. Ap chago, ap sugi jumok momtong jireugi
13. Ap sugi, palmok ulgool maki
14. Ap chago, ap sugi jumok momtong jireugi
15. Ap kubi, palmok arae maki
16. Ap kubi, jumok momtong jireugi, kihap

Choong Moo Form

1. Left back stance, high knifehand guarding block.
2. Right long stance, knifehand neck strike and knifehand high block.
3. Right back stance knifehand guarding block
4. Left long stance spearfinger strike to throat.
5. Left back stance guarding block.
6. Left crane stance, shin block.
7. Left back stance, guarding block
8. Skip, flying side kick (*kihap*) knifehand guarding block.
9. Left back stance knifehand low block
10. Left long stance, double knifehand neck strike.
11. Knee strike, itf turn, left long stance, right ridgehand with support.

12. Right side kick, left back kick, back stance forearm guarding block.
13. Left roundhouse kick, right back stance, pole block.
14. Jump backside 360, right back stance low knifehand guarding block.
15. Left long stance, right groin grab with support.
16. Right long stance (facing reverse) half mountain block
17. Right long stance, press block and spearfingers strike with support.
18. Spin, left back stance, reinforced middle block.
19. Horse stance, right out to in middle block with support, backfist.
20. Right side kick, left side kick, back stance middle knifehand block.
21. Left long stance, double palm uppercut
22. (ITF Turn), right long stance, right high block, left high punch (*kihap*)

Choong Moo Key Points

- You now have black on your belt, a color that will never leave!
- If you are old enough, start thinking about the possibility of having a career in martial arts.
- Start thinking about if you want to be a generalist or a specialist as a black belt.

Keep Notes to prepare for your black belt test:

Create three of your own One Step Sparring:

- 1)

- 2)

- 3)

Keep Notes to prepare for your black belt test:

CONGRATULATIONS! You've finally made it. This will be one of the most special moments in your life. Most of the questions have already been answered on the application, so feel free to keep page this for your personal records. (You can fill this out after your test.)

Name: Date of your Black Belt Test:

Board Breaks:

Name some friends/partners/instructors you tested with:

You're probably feeling many different emotions now. Describe some of them.

What are your overall impressions of the test?

What did you do well on?

What were you not happy with?

How have your goals changed since you started TKD?

Have you seen the benefits you were originally seeking?

1st Degree Black Belt is really only the beginning. What are your plans for the future?

Part 3: Appendix and References

In the recent past, martial artists were very guarded about their technique and many masters were convinced of the superiority of their own styles to the exclusion of all others. However, with the advent of the Internet and newfound openness in all areas of society, there has been a revolution of martial arts. Previously, some instructors would not train in other martial arts even if they knew that another art might provide better techniques for a given situation. This was often due to pride or ignorance of the other style. Now, however, forward-thinking martial artists borrow extensively from other styles and the KAT is no exception. While our main thrust has always been and will always be Traditional and Sport Taekwondo, for the Practical Self Defense Component we take groundwork from Brazilian Ju-Jitsu, throws and falls from Judo, and takedowns from wrestling. We also occasionally borrow techniques from other martial arts to help work on our balance and agility or to use for our demo team.

Here is a listing and brief summary of several other main martial arts. This is by no means a comprehensive list. Notice how many names of other martial arts contain the word 'Do.'

Aikido: Aikido is a Japanese martial art developed by Morihei Ueshiba (often referred to by his title 'O Sensei' or 'Great Teacher'). The main point of Aikido is to use an opponent's own force against him. The main techniques are throws and joint locks, and there are very few strikes. Aikido also places great emphasis on discipline and has ties with many philosophies of Zen Buddhism.

Boxing: Boxing has been practiced around the world for millennia.

It involves hitting another player with the fists only above the belt only. Boxing is a modern Olympic sport but in contrast to other Asian martial arts there is not much emphasis on discipline.

Brazilian Ju-Jitsu: Brazilian Ju-Jitsu has been most famously developed by the Gracie family. It is an offshoot of Japanese Ju-Jitsu that places more emphasis on the Guard position. This art places a high value on utility and is much less formal than other martial arts. They have been incredibly innovative and their technique has improved quickly throughout the last few decades. In tournaments where various styles compete against each other one on one, this style most clearly emerges the winner, unless strikers know enough of it to avoid takedowns and submissions.

Capoeira: Capoeira is a very interesting martial art developed in Brazil by slaves and former slaves from the Angolan region of Africa. In contrast to the other martial arts, Capoeira serves a more all-encompassing function. The call and response songs, use of instruments such as the *berimbau,* and multiple forms served as the slaves' only source of recreation, and entertainment and was a vehicle for transmission of culture.

A group of practitioners gathered around in a *Roda* (R is pronounced like H) and the man playing the *berimbau* played different tunes depending on whether the slavedrivers were around. The players changed their technique based on the rhythm he played such that they would hide or show their strikes depending on the situation.

Capoeira is very much like a dance, and uses many beautiful but less functional techniques. The fighting stance, or *jenga*, is different from other arts in that it is dynamic instead of static.

Hapkido: Hapkido literally means the "The art of coordinating energy." The founder of Hapkido, Choi, Yong Sul lived in Japan and trained with Japanese Ju-Jitsu masters during the occupation. Afterwards he returned to Korea and added more techniques from other Korean arts. Our step sparring comes from Hapkido. KAT students may also be able to get black belts in Hapkido.

Judo: Judo is a Japanese martial art developed by Jigoro Kano. It is similar to Ju-Jitsu, except that Judo took the dangerous techniques from Ju-Jitsu and 'softened' them. For instance, an arm break became a shoulder throw by turning the elbow. In this way they were able to train at full force without injuring each other. Judo is now a modern Olympic sport that consists mostly of throws. Groundfighting is stopped after ten seconds.

Karate-do: Karate literally means 'empty hand' and it is a Japanese martial art that has developed into one of the most popular in the world. In America, Karate schools usually compete in point sparring tournaments and are sometimes known for having excellent forms.

Kung Fu: Kung Fu is a Chinese martial art that encompasses many different styles. This is one of the oldest martial arts and it emphasizes conditioning, hand to hand grappling techniques, and sometimes acrobatic and esoteric kicks.

Muy Thai: Muy Thai, or Thai Kickboxing, is a martial art from Thailand. It is known for its brutal elbow, knee, and shin strikes and for its forward facing fighting stance. Thai kickboxers also condition their shins and other body parts extensively to destroy nerve endings and build up calluses and strong bones.

Ninjitsu: Ninjitsu was a style popular in feudal Japan. It was practiced by a secret group of assassins who dressed in black and tried to carry out their attacks in invisibility. Although at times groups of ninjas would try to overpower a target, a ninja's most successful attacks were the stealthiest. Often, they would simply dress in peasants' clothes and poison a lord's water supply or food. The most successful attack would not be seen as an attack at all, only an accident. When one imagines the fear that this caused in everyday people and the secrecy surrounding the ninja, it is no surprise that they were soon rumored to have supernatural powers. Isolated groups of people may practice Ninjitsu today, but it is a very small martial art, despite its popularity in movies.

Children who have parental support do much better in school and most other activities than those who do not. The fact that you signed your kids up for Taekwondo is a great first step. It shows that you are willing to invest time and money to help your children become confident, healthy, and happy. This guide was written to help busy parents like yourself know the best way to help.

Problems come not when parents become too involved, but when they become involved in the wrong way, put a disproportionate amount of pressure on their children to succeed, or get in fights with other parents. My favorite resource on this is the USA Hockey's group of Award Winning Public Service Announcements called *"Relax, it's just a game."* They can easily be found by Googling the name and USA Hockey.

Stress effort above results. With effort, results always come. Also, make sure that kids are having fun. Becoming an elite competitor in Taekwondo takes many years, and if it's not fun, kids won't stick with it. If they lost a match but made a new friend with their opponent, that's still a good thing. Lastly, remember that the rules of the dojang apply to everyone.

When trying to help your children, it helps to remember that there are three main components of training. There is a lot of overlap between the different components.

Traditional Taekwondo – Forms, etc. Used for getting belts and ranks

Sport Taekwondo – Sparring. Used for getting medals, tournaments.

Practical Self Defense – Grappling, other strikes. Used for defending yourself on street.

It's not the parents' job to teach their children Taekwondo (that's why you pay us!) but parents can do a lot to help their children in Taekwondo.

Parents can help their children in several main ways:

Help in training: Parents can hold paddles at home and in class, advise on forms, quiz students on Korean terminology, etc.

Motivational help: Parental support is one of the most important factors in children receiving their black belts and beyond.

Material Support: Paying for training, competitions, giving rides to class are all extremely important tasks for parents.

"When one of us succeeds, all of us succeed" is especially true of parents and their children in the martial arts.

About Taekwondo Competitions- Tournaments are usually all day affairs. They can seem frustrating and confusing, especially when one is unsure of the rules. Here are a few pointers that may help during tournament time.

Most tournaments will have several events. The two main events are forms and sparring (Olympic Style). The tournaments may also have board breaking, weapons forms, point style sparring, team sparring, creative forms, musical forms, demo competition, etc.

In general, the competition will proceed from events where you are least likely to hurt yourself to events where you are more likely to hurt yourself.

Forms

In the forms competition, two competitors will perform their forms at the same time. The judges will then give them a score. If there are three judges, they will use all the scores. If there are five judges, then they will throw out the highest and lowest score.

The scores are based on power, execution, balance, *kihap*, beginning and ending in the same spot, presence, etc. There is no objective scoring system. Judges are usually told to disregard slight stylistic differences between schools, ie, chambering, etc. That means if one school is all doing something small "wrong" the kids probably won't get scored up or down for it.

The judges mainly worry about being internally consistent within a division. Thus, if you got a 7.7 in one tournament and a 7.9 in the next it doesn't mean that your form is better now. Also if a black belt got an 8.0 and a blue belt got an 8.5 it doesn't mean the blue belt's form is better.

Sparring (Olympic Style)

Each tournament director will set the rules for his tournament. However, most of the rules are the same. The only thing that is different is usually who can use head contact and if it must be **light or full.**

Points are scored when one person kicks with any part of his foot to the scoring area on the hogu. Sound helps a lot in determining the points. If the attack is only partially blocked, a point may still score. There are usually three corner judges. If two of them press the score button within 1.5 seconds then a point goes up on the scoreboard. There may also be electronic hogus. The judges will then mainly score punches and head shots.

Oftentimes, the judges will not be that experienced and will be tired from referring all day. They are usually volunteers although sometimes they are paid or are black belts who get free entry. Even the highest rated referees in the world will miss points. Points often happen in the blink of an eye.

In many years of Colorado Taekwondo, there has been *very little outright cheating*. Often, the referees will miss your points, but they will miss your opponents' points the same amount on average.

When the corner judges miss an obvious head shot, the coach can quietly stand up and raise his hand. The center referee can then stop the match and poll the corner judges. Just because he does this does not mean the point will go up. The corner judges might not have seen it, the kick might have been to the neck or the back of the head, or the point might not have been valid. Remember, two out of three (or three out of four) must score the point for it to count.

The number of matches you will have will depend on the number of competitors in your division. Because of bye matches and the luck of the draw, the person who is third might be better than the person who is second in single elimination.

The main thing to remember is that tournaments are just vehicles that we have to make the kids better martial artists. Everyone wants to see their kid win. But a loss where they learn something might be much better for them than an easy win. Also, discipline is still the most important thing. The worst thing that can happen in a tournament is for a student to lose his cool and do something like yell at a ref, hit someone with a cheap shot, throw his helmet, etc. This reflects poorly on him and the school and parents. It's important for parents to always keep their cool too and to remember that when it's a matter of winning or losing, it's just a sport.

What you can do:
- Make sure the kids get a good night's sleep. This is important two nights before the tournament because they probably won't sleep well the night before anyway.
- Make sure that they eat well before and during the tournament. Not eating or drinking enough water in a long day can cause a loss of energy during the match.

- Make sure that they have all their equipment (helmet, shin and forearm protectors, instep protectors, mouthpiece, cup (males), hogu) water and any medicines that they need (inhalers), and that their fingernails and toenails are trimmed.
- Warm them up with kicking paddle drills and watch their form.
- Videotape the matches and let them analyze them later.
- For younger kids especially, make sure they are in the right ring (or holding area) at the right time.
- Cheer

Help in Training

Holding Paddles- Kicking paddles are an excellent and inexpensive training tool.
- Roundhouse Kick
    - Hold at either waist or head level.
    - Hold with laces down
    - Angle slightly toward kick
    - Provide a stiff kicking resistance.
- Ax Kick
    - Hold at head level
    - Hold with large section towards kicker
- General High Kick
    - Hold facing towards kicker at head level
    - Can be used for crescent kick, spin hook kick, high butterfly kick, 540, etc.

How to use them- First hold them steady, then vary timing, distance, height, frequency, stimulus reaction, combinations, etc.

Forms Training- You can help your kids *without knowing their form!*
Look for the same things they judge them on in the tournament.
- Balance, power, beginning and ending in the same spot, snap, etc. You can help them in these areas of their form.

- The same goes for One Step Sparring and Demonstration Forms

Korean Terminology- Quiz the kids on their terminology just as you would for their spelling words or other homework. They only have to memorize one group of words every three months.

Motivational Help

Successful kids in Taekwondo have parents who help to motivate them.

Your kids will get bored of Taekwondo.

Everyone will go through periods where they lose interest. For most this happens around green-blue belt. This is perfectly normal. It's even called the *"Blue belt blues."* **Taekwondo is hard.** Becoming good at these skills requires repetition of basic movements over and over until the body learns it. As instructors, we try to disguise this repetition so that students won't be bored. But it happens to everyone.

At this time, it is important for the parents to step in and help the children with perseverance. We live in a culture that is fixated on immediate gratification. We expect everything to be accomplished just the way we want it and we want it done yesterday. This is very dangerous. This kind of attitude leads to people dropping out of school, making bad financial decisions (i.e., buying things they can't afford), or just giving up on things when the going gets tough.

Children will do things for the moment and sacrifice the future. Most kids would stop going to school, never take a bath, or eat candy for every meal if their parents let them. It's the parents' job to make the kids do things that will help them in the future. In fact, that's one of the fundamental differences between children and adults.

It is very important that kids learn early on that achieving important things requires sacrifice, and sacrifice over time. Childhood is the best time to learn this. Parents have invested a lot of time and money in Taekwondo and parents don't want to see their kids lose interest either.

What can you do:

- Recognize that this is only temporary. Often it just takes a new belt, a new form, a new friend in class, or a great tournament to get back on track.
- Adjust the training schedule. Often burnout comes from kids attending too many classes. Other times, kids who attend too few classes will lose interest as they aren't seeing improvement.
- Try something new, i.e., weapons, demo, etc.
- For those in between ages, try switching between children's and adult classes.
- Set some short and long term goals. Accomplishing them will give more internal motivation.
- Remember that they will thank you when they finally achieve their black belt or competition goals.

Material Support

Bringing your children to class (or carpooling), paying for the lessons and competitions, and just helping them out overall is extremely important. While they might not realize how lucky they are now, they will definitely thank you for it when they are older.

C: Case Study: Pine Board Breaking in the Martial Arts

Today, people all over the world use martial arts for recreation, competition, and self defense. Over the years powerful techniques have been developed and cultivated and a popular way to show these techniques is to break pine boards.

Board breaking represents a large force applied to a piece of wood for a short time. Since both force and instantaneous striking velocity are important, the analysis was undertaken relative to breaking energy. The boards were assumed to be standard 12 in. x 12 in, x ¾ in. White Pine *(P. Strobus)* held tightly at both ends (all striking energy goes into breaking the board.) The board was assumed to be free of defects (no high local stress concentrations) and modeled according to column loading. This means that the maximum energy that the board can store before fractures begin to propagate is given by

$$U_{max}=V*\sigma_b/2E$$

where σ_b is the breaking stress, V is the board volume, and E is Young's Modulus. Since the boards are largely breaking in tension, σ_b can be replaced with M_r, the modulus of rupture. The modulus of rupture is the highest tensile stress a material can undergo in bending.

Figure 1 shows a 3D representation of the breaking energy applied to the board as a function of apparent mass (m_a) and striking speed. Apparent mass is a function of technique. For a punch, someone could punch with only their arm, or they could put their shoulder, hip, or whole body into the strike. Striking speed is defined as the instantaneous velocity of the limb at the point of contact with the board. The base case is a fresh pine board with a volume of 0.0017 m^3. With M_r=0.061 GN/m^2 and E=8.81 GN/m^2, the breaking energy is 359 J. The energy required to break the board is shown as a horizontal plane with z=359 J. Any combination of striking speed and apparent mass above this plane will result in fracture, any combination below the plane will result in a bruised limb.

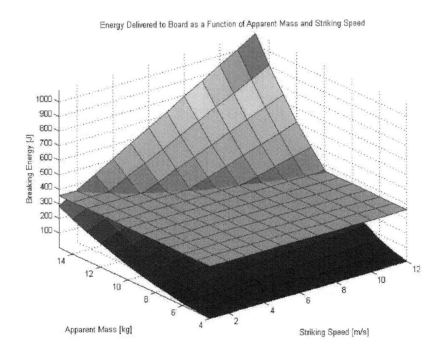

Figure 1. The energy delivered to a board is a function of striking speed and apparent mass. The horizontal plane represents the energy needed to break a standard adult board.

There are several recognized limitations with this analysis. First of all, the breaking stress energy is defined as the average energy per unit volume. During a strike, the stress energy is highly localized, and therefore neither shape nor geometry variations are adequately addressed. Secondly, at least some energy from the strike is used to move the board, and some is dissipated as heat and sound.

Overall, however, the predictions of the model are consistent with experiential evidence, and provide a meaningful estimate of parameters that can determine whether a given board will break or not.

Breaking of Boards Under Non-Idealized Holding Conditions

The above analysis could be considered a 'best case' scenario for breaking boards. In reality, however, even the best holders will move the board slightly. Also, many higher ranking students break a board that is held only at one end. How does this affect the required breaking energy?

One Handed Holds- **Now the board is modeled as a cantilever beam. The martial artist must deliver enough energy to cause any deflections of the board in addition to the energy to break the board. This will be equal to the displacement of the beam multiplied by the force applied to cause that displacement. With a point load P applied in the middle of the board, the maximum deflection is given by:**

$$D=5PL^3/(24EI)$$

Assuming that the deflection is small and linear, multiplying this by the force that caused this displacement will give a reasonable approximation to the energy 'wasted' in this manner. Since E= force times distance, now the energy delivered to a board during a particular strike is:

$$E=1/2m_av^2 - 5P^2L^3/(24EI)$$

But how do we find P? For this analysis we consider the impulse applied to the board. Since its original momentum is zero, we have the momentum of the strike (m_av) equal to the force of the strike multiplied by the time of application. Here the time of application is taken to be 0.25 s. This leads to the final equation for a one sided hold:

$$E=1/2m_av^2 - 5(m_av)L^3/(6EI)$$

However, for the given parameters over a normal range of strikes, less than one joule is lost to move the board, which moves only 7 mm. In reality, a perfectly fixed cantilever beam is an unrealistic assumption. A loosely held board sweeps out a quarter circle with a radius of its length, so the average board particle moves pi*L/8 meters. A better equation is graphed in figure 2.

$$E=1/2m_av^2 - (m_av)L*pi/2$$

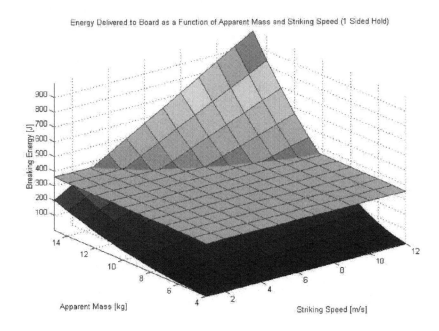

Energy Delivered to Board as a Function of Apparent Mass and Striking Speed (1 Sided Hold)

Figure 2. The energy delivered to a board is a function of striking speed and apparent mass for a one handed hold. Note that now the horizontal plane covers more of the breaking energy curve, signifying a more difficult break.

Two Sided Holds- A two sided hold in which the holders give can be modeled in several different ways. The amount that they give could be expressed as a fixed distance, or a fixed or percentage amount of energy or force absorbed. A percentage of the force absorbed is the best option, because the holders are applying a force, this will let the distance that the board moves be a function of the strike. With F as a fraction of the force absorbed by the holders, the board now feels the net force Fnet=(1-F)(m_av)/0.25 s, which gives an acceleration to the board of Fnet/m_b. Since the board has this acceleration for the same 0.25 s and W=Fnet*1/2a_b*t2, the energy imparted to the board in a strike is:

$$E = 1/2m_a v^2 - ((1-F)(m_a v))^2 / 2 m_b$$

The results are plotted in figure 3 (F=0.80) and figure 4 (F=0.85). In general, for F values greater than 0.9 the difference is small. For 0.78<F<0.9 the difference becomes marked, and only a very powerful strike can fracture the board. Below this range the model breaks down as the board undergoes an acceleration that causes it to go away from the strike faster than the strike itself, so the board cannot be broken regardless of the strike. It is interesting to note that this model can also handle F values slightly greater than one, as when an adult will push a board against a child's strike to make it easier for them to break.

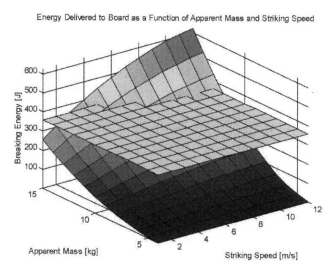

Energy Delivered to Board as a Function of Apparent Mass and Striking Speed

Figure 3. The energy delivered to a board is a function of striking speed and apparent mass for a two handed hold where the holders absorb 80% of the force. Note that now the horizontal plane covers most of the breaking energy curve, signifying a very difficult break.

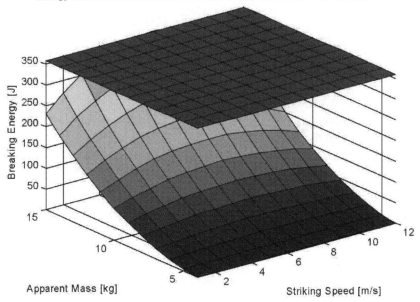

Figure 4. The energy delivered to a board is a function of striking speed and apparent mass for a two handed hold where the holders absorb 85% of the force. Note that now the horizontal plane covers most of the breaking energy curve, signifying a near impossible break.

With proper training, board breaking is an excellent way to demonstrate the beauty, power, and grace in martial arts and a scientific understanding of the mechanics behind it can greatly aid the martial artist.

D: Demonstration Techniques
(Trick Kicks)

Demonstration techniques are the techniques that look very impressive, but probably wouldn't work in a real fight or match. These aren't to be confused with the demonstration forms (1-6) that are required for belt testing. Demo techniques are not a required part of the curriculum, but they are good to learn as they are fun, challenging, and can help you understand concepts used in the regular techniques.

However, demonstration techniques can be dangerous if they are not learned properly. **These techniques often go higher, faster, and more inverted than the regular techniques.** Also, there are not as many qualified teachers for demo techniques. Make sure that you have proper instructors and pads when trying new demo techniques. We have made the following step by step guides for learning a few common demo techniques.

The following guide just goes over the basics. See the DVD for videos of the techniques.

Path 1: Z and X Axis Spinning Techniques.

1. **Basics** – First you must learn the basic kicks like roundhouse and spin hook.
2. **Reverse Step, roundhouse** – You will kick with the front foot after doing a reverse step.
3. **Butterfly kick** – The butterfly kick involves jumping right before you kick.
4. **Raize** – This is like a butterfly kick but there is no kick. You should concentrate on going as high as possible.
5. **540 Degree Kick** – The next step is to do the butterfly kick and land on the kicking foot.
6. **Swipe** – This kick is a 540 at where your body rotates on the X axis instead of the normal Z axis.

7. **540 Degree Hook Kick** – Now you use the other foot that didn't land and do a hook kick with it.
8. **720 Kicks** – Now you can do any of the above with modifications or multiple kicks.

Path 2: Y Axis Spinning Techniques

1. **Kung Fu Butterfly Kick** – In this kick you will first do a reverse step and then jump upwards, keeping your chest parallel to the floor. You will land on the opposite foot you take off from (180 aerial spin)
2. **Butterfly Twist** – Now you will land on the same foot that you take off with. It's important to jump high and spin quickly. (360 aerial spin)
3. **Hypertwist** – This time you will come around again and land on the opposite foot you took off with. (540 aerial spin)
4. **Corkscrew Twist** – You bring your leg up as if going for an upwards kick and then jump and do the twist in the air. (360 aerial spin)

Path 3: Forwards Tumbling

1. **Front Roll** (Grappling Drill A)
2. **Dive Roll** – Try to go over higher and higher obstacles. Make sure that you roll diagonally at 45 degrees and spread the force of the fall out.
3. **Front Flip Tuck**- Now you will flip over and go from feet to feet. Make sure to tuck tightly.
4. **Brandi** – This is a front flip with a half twist.
5. **Webster** – This one starts out with an ax kick and you use the momentum to raise your body upwards enough to flip.

E: Ten Influential Martial Artists (& One Philosopher)

The martial arts that we practice today have been influenced by literally millions of people down through the ages. The following is a list of eleven people (ten martial artists and one philosopher) who have been some of the most influential. Of course, any list such as this is subject to debate, and the figures below have each been the subject of many entire books. However, knowing a little bit about each and their contributions will help students to understand the current state of our training. It is important to know how our training became like it is today and also to have role models. When you feel adversity in your life, it is helpful to see what other people have been able to overcome.

Confucius (~550 BC) – Confucius was not a martial artist, but his teachings did much to influence Asian society and thought. His main teachings were about the **Five Relationships** - between father and son, husband and wife, prince and subject, elder and youngster, and friends. Each person in a relationship has a duty to the other. This shows in the relationships that we have in our martial arts schools.

Bodhidharma (~500 AD) – Bodhidharma was an Indian monk who migrated to China in the 6th century AD. There are a lot of myths and legends surrounding him, and the truth is hard to ascertain. However, the legend is that the monks of the time were physically unable to deal with the strict meditation regimen that Buddhism requires. He purportedly stared at a wall for nine years without speaking. Seven years into his nine, he fell asleep. After this he cut off his own eyelids so it would not happen again. Finally, he understood how martial arts practice could help.

According to Jeffrey Broughton's *The Bodhidharma Anthology: The Earliest Records of Zen*, there is another legend about a time when Bodhidharma spoke with the emperor.

The emperor asked Bodhidharma, *"What is the highest meaning of noble truth?"*
Bodhidharma answered, *"There is no noble truth."*

The emperor then asked Bodhidharma, *"Who is standing before me?"* Bodhidharma answered, *"I don't know."*

The emperor then asked Bodhidharma, *"How much karmic merit have I earned by ordaining Buddhist monks, building monasteries, having sutras copied, and commissioning Buddha images?"*

Bodhidharma answered, *"None."*

Regardless of the truth of these legends, the important point is that the beginning of the martial arts as we know it can be traced to the moment when someone decided to combine a higher spiritual purpose with fighting. People have fought since the beginning of history, but having the martial arts be more than just fighting is something that originally happened when people decided to add other elements to basic technique.

Miyamoto Mushashi (1584-1645) – Miyamoto Mushashi is a famous swordsman from Japan's feudal era. He is most famous for his book *"A Book of Five Rings,"* called in Japanese *Go Rin No Sho.* He was orphaned at age 7 and when he was only 13, he was challenged by an accomplished samurai. The samurai was armed with a sword and Mushashi only had a stick. Mushashi won the duel, and from that point on, he lived by wandering around the land challenging whoever he could find and seeking enlightenment by way of the sword. He fought in more than 60 duels and six wars, and ended up dying of old age in a cave.

His skill with the blade was so great that he often would only bring a *bokken* (wooden practice sword) to a duel when his opponents would bring swords and spears.

Mushashi was a strange character. After being attacked in a bathhouse and having to fight his way out, he never took another bath for the last few decades of his life. He traveled around in tattered rags and had oily, unkempt hair. Yet, his poetry and calligraphy are some of the most valued of any Japanese artist.

He is considered by many to be the greatest swordsman who ever lived.

Jigoro Kano (1860 -1938) – Jigoro Kano was born into a tumultuous time as Japan was just becoming open to the west after the Meiji Restoration. Jigoro wanted to study martial arts all his life, which is not surprising considering that in his teens he was a 5 foot 2 inch, 90 pound weakling who was beaten up by bullies all the time. However, he didn't start training until he was almost 18 years old.

Kano was very open to different ideas about martial arts and education in general. He took ideas from other styles, western wrestling and boxing, and science and physics. He changed the jujitsu of the day by making it less dangerous. That way, his students could practice on a fully resisting partner instead of just practicing forms. At age 22, only 4 years after he started training, he founded the Kodokan school and the martial art of Judo. The school is one of the oldest surviving martial arts schools, about to celebrate its 125th birthday. Branches have sprung up all over the world. Other innovations that Kano had at the Kodokan were the use of a colored belt system to denote different classes of trainees and the systemization and teaching of the falling technique to beginning students.

Kano was a very busy man. By the time he was 25, he had not only graduated college, but was already a professor and the headmaster of two different universities, in addition to the Kodokan. He was also the first Japanese member of the International Olympic Committee.

Masahiko Kimura (1917-1993) – Kimura was one of Kodokan Judo's most famous students. He helped to popularize Judo by spreading it around the world in a series of famous matches in the mid 20th Century.

Judo of the period was different from most martial arts today, in that advancement in rank was determined only by beating people higher ranked than you, rather than minimum age or time. Thus, Kimura became the youngest ever 5th *Dan* at age 18. That same year, he lost four matches. Those would be the only four matches that he ever lost in his life. Later on, he would go on to hunt down all of the people who had bested him and defeat all of them.

His dominance was so strong that he would do things like have a strenuous 3 hour sparring session before showing up at the national championship to soundly defeat all his opponents.

Kimura was a bear of a man who did hundreds of pushups daily and simply overpowered many of his opponents. One of his most famous matches was against Helio Gracie. In this match, Kimura manhandled the much smaller Gracie. At one point, Kimura had his legs on Gracie's chest and caused Gracie to go unconscious. Later on, when Kimura shifted, Gracie revived and continued the match! The match ended when Kimura went to lock Gracie's shoulder. Gracie refused to tap, so his corner threw in the towel.

The match ended with mutual respect from both sides. In honor of Kimura's fight, Gracie named the lock that defeated him the Kimura lock in Gracie jujitsu.

Helio Gracie (1913- 2009) – Helio Gracie was a Brazilian man who was sickly as a child. He tried to learn jujitsu, but found that many of the techniques were not suited to his small frame. Thus, he modified the techniques to require an even smaller amount of leverage. He also made good use of the guard position, which was used in Judo but only sparingly. He recognized the value that the guard can have for a smaller person.

Although Gracie's fight career was nowhere near as prolific as that of his sons, he did have his share of marathon matches. He fought one match for fourteen ten minute rounds before it was stopped by police. He also holds the record for the longest match, one that he fought against his former student and lost by knockout from a kick to the head after an amazing 3 hours and 40 minutes!

Choi Hong Hi (1918-2002) – General Choi was another person who was sick as a child. He grew up during the Japanese occupation of Korea and thus learned Japanese Karate techniques. One time, the Japanese put him in jail for a nationalist Korean disturbance, and he taught Karate to the inmates and guards.

General Choi was in the Korean army and rose to the rank of Major-General. He also served as the country's ambassador to Malaysia. General Choi was the person who first suggested the name of Taekwondo when the art was being brought together in the 1950s and 1960s. He served as the head of the International Taekwondo Federation (ITF) for many years, eventually moving to Canada.

Bruce Lee (1940-1973) – Bruce Lee is one of the best known martial artists. His influence is important in a number of ways that might not be known to everyone. First of all, he was a movie star who made several classic films. This helped to popularize martial arts in many other parts of the world besides Asia. It also showed studios that martial arts movies could be profitable. For instance, *Enter the Dragon* cost less than $1 million and made over $90 million! This helped pave the way for other martial arts movies and movie stars, which in turn led to many more people starting to train.

Another way that Lee was influential was his emphasis on physical conditioning. He was able to do one handed pushups on two fingers and was very strong and powerful for his size. He also was the inventor of the style of Jeet Kun Do, and emphasized free flowing arts over classical, more structured arts. In this way he was a forerunner of the MMA revolution that happened after his death.

Jhoon Rhee (1932- Present) – In the second half of the 20th century, many Korean masters went all around the world to spread Taekwondo. One of the most influential in the US was Jhoon Rhee. Rhee has taught many people, including over 300 US Congressmen. He was also one of the first people to ever set a form to music.

Rhee was instrumental in systematizing the business of school operation. Many masters before this time had no grasp of business or organization building, and as a result classes were small and schools often closed. Perhaps his greatest achievement was the invention of the RheeMax foam sparring gear, which allowed people all over the world to train harder with reduced injuries.

Ernie Reyes, Sr. (1947- Present) – Ernie Reyes is a great martial arts master from California. His *West Coast Action Team* was instrumental in pushing the boundaries of creative martial arts and demonstration techniques. This demo team is also quite possibly the most impressive demo team in the world. Reyes and his children also starred in several Hollywood movies.

Reyes is also very active in organization building. He is a fantastic motivator and dynamic performer and speaker. He is also the creator of the Little Dragons curriculum, a method for teaching martial arts to preschool age children.

Lopez Family (Present Time) – The Lopez family have dominated Sport Taekwondo like no other family. In 2005 when all three won the world championship, the USOC stated that never in the history of the US has one family dominated any sport in such a manner. Jean Lopez is the oldest brother, and he is their coach. He also won a silver medal in the world championships. Steven is arguably the best Taekwondo player ever. He lost only one match from 1999-2008, including in his streak 2 Olympic gold medals and 3 world championship gold medals. He is the only player to win 5 world championships. Mark was the youngest man from any country to win a medal in the world championships— he has one each of gold, silver, and bronze. Sister Diana was not to be outdone, and took her own gold medal in the world championship. In the 2008 Olympics, all three siblings won medals. It should be noted that in April, 2018, Jean Lopez was suspended from USAT due to alleged abuse of athletes he was coaching.

Looking at this list, several things are striking. One is how many famous martial artists were small, sick, and picked on as children. Certainly, these early experiences helped to mold them into fierce fighters. Another thing to notice about the list is the lack of diversity. Long ago, martial arts training was reserved for nobles and their sons or the elite in the military. Through the work of many on this list, the number of people training has increased incredibly. Now, we have recognized the positive impact martial arts can have on all people. At many schools there is special training for very young children, older men and women, the disabled, mentally and physically handicapped people, etc. One hundred years from now, we are likely to see many of these people on a new list.

F: Weapons

Weapons training is not one of the three critical components that make up the core of our school. However, training in traditional weapons still has much value to any martial artist for several reasons:

- Weapons can give an advantage to a smaller, weaker, or disabled person.
- Since the principles behind armed and unarmed combat are the same, weapons training can help you understand your unarmed techniques on a deeper level.
- Weapons training is an important social and cultural part of our martial arts heritage.

All Weapons

Safety

Before continuing, a word of strong caution is in order. In order to train safely and effectively with weapons, your discipline must be even higher than normal. Training with weapons, even dull, wooden or padded ones, can be very dangerous. You have the potential to hurt yourself or others. This is why weapons training was considered very sacred in many cultures. Here are some important things to keep in mind:

- Always make sure you are practicing in a clear area.
- Make sure your weapon is secure and in good repair. The last thing you want is your weapon to break and part of it to go flying at your partner.
- Practice difficult or blind techniques with padded weapons first.

- **Never** do contact training with sharp weapons.

Basics

Unlike unarmed fighting, weapons add many different dimensions to training. For instance, we now have armed vs. unarmed combat and armed vs. armed. We also have a myriad of different weapons to contend with. What if it's sword vs. spear? Or Bo vs. nunchuks? Naginata vs. fan? How can we practice techniques that will help us in every conceivable situation? Projectile weapons (stars, blowgun, bow and arrows) are a separate case and will be considered differently later on. However, our school has come up with the following way to teach weapons techniques.

With limited exceptions, the striking weapon itself doesn't matter as much as the direction of the strike. This is true for both attacking and defending. No matter what weapon you have, you are always trying to make certain basic strikes that attack vital target areas.

Thus, our school has come up with ten basic strikes, depicted in the picture below. The 9 strike is a straight forward thrusting strike and the 10 strike is a flick strike to the opponent's hands.

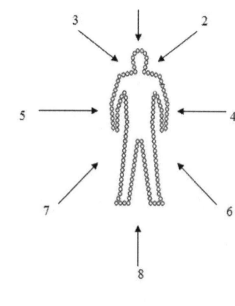

Each strike also has a corresponding block. For instance, a 3 strike with any weapon can be defended by a 3 block with any weapon. Note that the angle of the strike takes precedence over the target. For instance, a straight strike to the side of the neck would be a high 4 strike, not a 2 strike.

Traditionally, weapons were not taught differently for people who were left handed. The reason is that an opposite body strike (3,5,7) will be executed like a same body strike (2,4,6) for a left handed vs. right handed person. The actual technique will be reversed. Thus, a right handed person will do a 3 strike with the same mechanics as a left handed one does a 2 strike.

Now that each weapon has these 10 basic attacks and blocks, we also need to fill out other basic protocol techniques. Namely, each weapon needs to have a grip, an attention stance, a ready stance, and a way to go back to ready stance.

Each weapon may have other strikes and techniques unique to that weapon. For instance, the sword has drawing, sheathing, disarming, and cleaning techniques. The weapon may also have trick moves such as spins, releases, figure 8s, roles, fakes, etc.

Each weapon also needs a **base form**. This form is simply a repetition of basic moves in a sequence to help you learn them. Sometimes the base forms can be done with partners.

Next, most weapons will have a **partner form**. This form is actually two separate forms that when done together with a partner will make a fighting scene. Care must be used to avoid hitting the partner.

Finally, each weapon will have one or many **competition forms**. These forms are to be used directly in weapons form competition and will include many more flashy moves. In contrast to the other forms, these competition forms may be customized and personalized to fit each individual performing them.

Sword

History: Swords have been part of nearly every human culture since the bronze age. They come in many different shapes and sizes. The main sword that we practice with is the curved Japanese style long sword, called a Katana, Tachi, or even 'samurai sword." The art involved with drawing, cutting, and using this sword is known as Iaido.

Kendo, literally, "The Way of the Sword" is a martial art associated with sword practice. There is a similar Korean martial art known as Headong Gumdo. This art uses more innovative movements including spins and kicks. We will use techniques from both arts at KAT.

Sword Types:

Katana: These are the razor sharp curved medal blades of legend. These swords have been used in Japan for hundreds of years. However, their use in our context will be rare because of the danger involved in wielding them. Modern, mass-produced Katana are usually made of one piece of medal cast into a mold. However, the traditional, high quality swords are made from two different pieces of metal. One is strong but does not hold an edge well while the other can be sharpened but is brittle. Swordsmiths would fold the first metal together with the second so the result is a sword that is both strong and sharp.

Bokken: These are wooden replicas of katanas. Traditionally, a young samurai boy would receive a bokken on his fifth birthday and begin his training. These swords are excellent to use in forms practice, but still too dangerous to use on a partner, even with armor.

Shinai: Shinai are straight swords made from four pieces of bamboo material. While their straightness is a disadvantage for those wishing to learn to use curved swords, because they collapse on impact, they absorb most of the force of a blow. Thus, the art of Kendo permits two competitors to strike each other with shinai as long as both of them are wearing full armor (bogu.)

Shinai also have a yellow string. This string signifies the reverse of the cutting edge.

Fitting: Kendo competition rules proscribe the size and weight of a shinai based on the age of the player. However, a good approximation is that if you place the shinai point down on the floor, the end of the tsuka (handle) should come up to your sternum.

Grip: The proper grip on the sword is very important to ensure that power is evenly transferred through the blade. In general, you want to grip with your right hand near the sword guard (tusba) and your left hand on the base of the handle. You want your hands to be as far apart as possible, as this will help you direct power through the blade. In general, your right hand will act as a guide while the pulling action of your left hand will do most of the work.

Attention Stance: In the attention stance, the sword is held at the left side. This can be done by placing the sword in your belt or in its scabbard, or simply holding the sword with the left hand.

Bow: The standard bow is done by bringing the right hand up over the heart with a push block motion while bowing. There is also a sitting bow called sankyo which is often exchanged in kendo.

Ready Stance: The ready stance is known as *Chudan no kamae.* Your feet are spread as in walking stance, with the heel of the rear leg raised up off the floor. Your left hand is even with your belt, and the point of the sword is leveled at your opponent's eyes.

Basic Form: The basic form is a partner form where two partners face each other. One leads with strikes 1-9 while moving forward while the other counters with blocks 1-9 while moving backwards. After the last 9 block the partner who blocked will counter with 9 strike (tsuki strike).

Partner Form: There are 10 partner forms from Kendo that originated in the early 1900s. Seven of the forms are with the long sword (tachi) and three are with the short sword (kodachi). These 10 forms are mastered by a 1st degree black belt in Kendo.

Competition Form: The first competition/demo form is the partner form from the demo team. The next competition form is the 3rd Degree black belt form from Headong Gumdo.

Tricks: There are many sword tricks available, including spins and releases.

Special Techniques: Special techniques of the sword include cutting, drawing, and sheathing techniques.

Blade Cleaning Techniques: (Chiburi) Swords also require a blade cleaning technique known as chiburi. Once a sword has made a cut, the swordsman must clean the blade before it is resheathed. Otherwise, the scabbard would be very difficult to clean. Usually, this is just a strong flick of the wrist to remove dirt and blood from the blade. After a battle was finished, more elaborate cleaning rituals were observed.

Nunchuks

History: The Nunchuks Wikipedia entry states:

Although the certain origin of nunchaku is not known, it was possibly invented in Okinawa. The popular belief is that the nunchaku was originally a short flail used to thresh rice (separate the grain from the husk). However some say that this weapon was not developed from a grain flail, and was created by a martial artist looking for a way to conceal his staff from the current oppressive government so he decided to cut it into three sections. The three sectioned staff is commonly known today as the sansetsukon. The nunchaku was derived from this, over time becoming what it is today.

Its development as a weapon supposedly grew out of the moratorium on edged weaponry under the Satsuma daimyo due to their restrictive policy of weapons control after invading Okinawa in the 17th century. (Some maintain that the weapon was most likely conceived and used exclusively for that end, as the configuration of actual flails and bits are unwieldy for weapons use, not to mention the fact that peasant farmers were unlikely to train for 'improvised' combat against professional warriors.) The modern nunchaku has been modified for its use as a weapon and would make a relatively ineffective rice flail.

Types: Nunchuks come in many different types. The staves can be made out of wood (rattan, cherry, bamboo) or more recently plastic and aluminum. The chain connecting them can be a string or chain links connected with ball bearings. Finally, in modern times the ends can even be made to hold glowsticks or electronic lights.

Fitting: The length of each piece should roughly be the length of your forearm. The chain should be fitted by letting the nunchuks hang over the side of your hand with the palm facing downward. Both ends should point straight down, with no extra chain.

Grip: The nunchuks should be gripped firmly in one hand. A grip near the chain will give you maximum control and minimum range, while a grip near the end will give you minimum control and maximum range. Thus, you may be required to switch grips during a form or fight.

Attention Stance: In the attention stance you grip the nunchuks in your left hand and do a normal attention stance.

Bow: Keep the nunchuks in your left hand and bow by placing your right hand forward over your heart.

Ready Stance: The ready stance is like a normal stance except you hold one end of each nunchuk in each hand.

Basic Form: See the DVD for the nunchuks basic form.

Partner Form: There is no partner form for nunchuks.

Competition Form: The nunchuks competition form is still under development.

Tricks: Tricks with the nunchuks involve spins, hand switches, and chain techniques.

Bo Staff

History: The Bo staff is one of the oldest and most versatile weapons. Ever since one cave man hit another with a downed tree branch, man has used and refined the staff.

Types: Most staffs are made of a long, thin piece of wood. They may also be made of metal, plastic, or foam. Some staffs are tapered at the end. These are for spinning quickly, and will not be of much use against another weapon. Staffs might also have something on the end, such as a mop, broom, or spear. The KAT staff techniques are taught so that they will work with a spear as well.

Fitting: The general rule is that staffs should be a few inches higher than the user, up to 6 feet high.

Grip: The staff may be gripped in various ways, but the most common way is to grip it so that your hands divide it into thirds. The forward hand will be facing palm up, while the back hand will face palm down.

Attention Stance: The attention stance is with the staff in the left hand and held out from the body at a 45 degree angle.

Bow: When you bow with the staff, let it come out to the left side at 45 degrees and bring your right hand up towards your chest.

Ready Stance: In the ready stance you have your right foot in the front and hold the staff in the grip described above.

Basic Form: See the DVD for the basic form.

Partner Form: The basic partner form involves attacking with strikes 1-9 and countering, as with the sword form.

Competition Form: The competition form is still under development.

Tricks and Special Techniques: Tricks and special techniques include spins, block to strike combinations, and aerial moves.

Recommended Reading

Although this handbook has a large amount of information, it is only the beginning of your studies of the martial arts. The following books and websites are recommended for more information.

Books

Taekwondo: State of the Art: Master Sun Chul Whang and Jun Chul Whang

Fighting Science: Martina Spraque

The Tao of Jeet Kun Do: Bruce Lee

A Book of Five Rings: Miyamoto Mushashi

The Art of War: Sun Tzu

Taekwondo Associations

There are several important Taekwondo associations. Worldwide, the **World Taekwondo Federation (WTF)** and **International Taekwondo Federation (ITF)** compete with each other. Domestically, there are two major organizations, **USA Taekwondo (USAT)**, and the **Amateur Athletic Union (AAU)**.

World Taekwondo Federation (WTF) - The WTF is headquartered at the Kukkiwon in Korea and is the main authority for the teaching of Taekwondo worldwide. Founded in 1972, the WTF has over 180 member nations and was led by Dr. Kim Un-Young, who also served as vice president of the **International Olympic Committee (IOC)** until 2004. The current WTF head is

Dr. Chung Won Choue. The WTF is also the official representative of the Sport Taekwondo style in the Olympic Games. As a school, we follow the WTF sparring rules for Olympic Style Sparring.

www.wtf.org

International Taekwondo Federation (ITF) - The ITF is located in Canada and until recently was headed by General Choi Hong Hi. It is a more traditional style of Taekwondo that emphasizes control and power. After his death, the ITF split into three competing organizations.

www.tkd-itf.org

United States Taekwondo (USAT) - The USAT is the governing body for Taekwondo in the United States. They set the process for determining national champions and the official national team. The internet address is:

www.usa-taekwondo.us

Amateur Athletic Union (AAU) - The AAU is a multi-sport organization that has one part dedicated to Taekwondo. They hold their own national championship. They also include point sparring in their tournaments.

www.aautaekwondo.com

National Collegiate Taekwondo Association (NCTA) - The NCTA is nearly thirty years old. It is in charge of the National Collegiate Championships that happen each year. This is a qualifier to compete for the US collegiate team. In 2010 KAT hosted the Championships, which was the first time it was held in Colorado.

www.ncta-usa.com

(FISU) - The FISU is the international collegiate sports governing body. In order to compete, participants must be university students in their respective country and be on their country's collegiate team.

www.fisu.net

My Testing Table

Name: Date I started:

Belt Color	Date	Notes
White to Yellow belt		
Yellow to High Yellow		
High Yellow to Green		
Green to High Green		
High Green to Blue		Half way to black belt!
Blue to High Blue		
High Blue to Red		
Red to High Red		
High Red to Dbl Black Stripe Red		
Dbl Black Stripe Red to Black Belt		
1st *Dan* to 2nd *Dan* Black		
2nd *Dan* to 3rd *Dan* Black		
3rd *Dan* to 4th *Dan* Black		Add *Master* to taekwondo title!
4th *Dan* to 5th *Dan* Black		

Progress Table

Fill in the table with your best effort. See how this improves over time.

Rank	Time for 10 kicks w/ one leg	Time for 100 Double Kicks	Best Form	Pushups in 1 minute	Situps in 1 minute
10th *Gup*					
9th *Gup*					
8th *Gup*					
7th *Gup*					
6th *Gup*					
5th *Gup*					
4th *Gup*					
3rd *Gup*					
2nd *Gup*					
1st *Gup*					
1st *Dan*					
2nd *Dan*					
3rd *Dan*					
4th *Dan*					

Tournament Record

Fill out the following grid after each tournament to keep a record. The online forms will automatically calculate and graph statistics.

Tournament	Date	Won	Lost	Medals	Notes (who you went against, did well on...etc.)

KAT Patches

KAT students may wear patches on their uniform if they earn them.

K A T – Goes on the back part of the dobak (butt flap). The bottom of the letters should be 1 inch up from the Adidas mark and centered. There should be 1 inch in between each letter.

KAT Tiger Patch (or wolf/ACT) Should go on the left chest over the heart, even with and opposite to the Adidas mark on the other side.

KAT Competition Team Patch – Should go on the left shoulder, 1 inch down from the seam. That way, when your right leg is in the back, your opponent gets to be intimidated by what team you are on ☺.

Numbers – Should go on the right shoulder, 1 inch down from the red/black Adidas Taekwondo mark.

Captain's C – Should go one inch under the competition team patch.

Preheat garment up for 15 sec. with iron. Cover letter/# with fine cloth over garment and press letter on garment firmly with iron for 25 sec. A few security stitches may help secure letters.

Other Patches
Other patches can be sewn on the gear bag or on each arm going downwards in the order you earned them.

- **KAT Tournament -** Successfully compete in the KAT White Tiger Martial Arts Championships

- **KAT Mountain Training -** Climb to the top of a 14,000 ft mountain with the school

- **KAT Survival Training** - Score at least 75 points on the survival training weekend.

- **KAT Summer Camp** -Attend summer camp and earn at least 7 beads.
- **USAF Falcon Trail -** Hike the entire length of trail (more than 1 day may be used). Identify 10 species of plants and animals, and perform 30 mins of conservation work..

- **Full Splits Club -** Do 180 Degree splits and take picture

- **Junior Instructor -** Complete Level I Instructor Training. No Charge

- **Instructor -** Complete Level II Instructor Training. No Charge.

- **Senior Instructor -** Complete Level III Instructor Training. No Charge.

- **KAT Patch -** All students may wear.

- **ACT Patch -** Students of Auraria Campus Taekwondo may wear.

- **Old KAT Patch -** Attend 350 Classes.

- **USA / Korea Patch -** All students may wear

KAT Belt Privileges

White Belt – Now officially a student. Can attend beginners classes.

Yellow Belt – Can attend boxing, grappling, and demo team classes. Can play battle chess.

High Yellow Belt – Can begin sparring training and join competition team. 8 year olds and above can attend weapons class if they show good discipline. Can begin to attend Level 2 class.

Green Belt – Officially graduate from Level 1 class. Eligible to participate in the Future Black Belt Program.

High Green Belt – Can use submissions in free grappling (children).

Blue Belt – Can begin Instructor Training class.

High Blue Belt – Can attend *Dan* Test Prep Class.

Red Belt – Eligible to try out for Elite Demo Team. Now an advanced belt.

High Red Belt – Can become Level 1: Assistant Instructor.

Double Stripe Red Belt – Earn free private planning sessions to work on your black belt test.

1st *Dan* **Black Belt** – Earns the *You Dan Ja* title. Can learn *Ho Rang Ee* form. Can learn all black belt forms in sport poomsae class.

2nd *Dan* **Black Belt** - Can become Level 2: Instructor.

3rd *Dan* **Black Belt** - Can become Level 3: Senior Instructor.

4th *Dan* **Black Belt** - Earns the *Sa Bum Nim* (Master) title.

8th *Dan* **Black Belt** – Earns the *Kwan Jang Nim* (Grandmaster) title.

H: Quick Curriculum Summary

The following tables show which requirements each belt must know in order to advance to the next belt.

Note for Satellite Program Students: Certain of these requirements may be taught on a rotating basis (i.e., several different belts learning the same requirement) to facilitate learning and testing.

All students may be asked to demonstrate kicking and hand technique line drills and board breaking. An essay on the word of the month is also required. (Except Metro Students)

Everyone must have a clean uniform and properly tied belt.

Everyone must know basic school and Taekwondo history.

Green and above may be asked to demonstrate free sparring and free grappling.

There is a three month training period between all belts except for white belts (minimum 2 weeks) and Double Black Stripes (minimum 6 months)

Modifications for Students Under 7 years old

G: Show shrimping and bridging escapes from mount
1-10: Show submission setup only
OSS: Not required.
Waiting Period: 4.5 months required as yellow and high yellow belts.

Requirement Tables

Little Tigers Testing Requirements

Note that time limits are approximate, due to the scheduling of tests.

Belt Color	Requirement	Safety Requirement
White	Attention Stance, Listening Stance, Proper Sitting, Ready Stance, Sparring Stance, Bow, Enter and exit the dojang	
White with Yellow Stripe	Falling Technique from sitting (Left, Right, Back, Front)	Safety Stance
White with Green Stripe	Front Kick, Roundhouse Kick, Side Kick, Crescent Kicks, Ax Kick	Crossing Street
White with Blue Stripe	Demonstration 1	Stranger Danger
White Belt with Red Stripe	First 8 moves of Chun Ji	Parent Phone Number
White Belt with Red Stripe with Yellow Horizontal Stripe	Full white belt requirements	What is 911

KAT Color Belt Requirements

Belt Color	Form	Terminology	Demo	Grappling	One Steps
White	Chun-Ji	Basics	1	**A:** Falling **B:** Rolling	
Yellow	TG1	Basics Part 2	2	**C:** Underhooks **D:** Riding back	#1-3
Green Stripe	TG2	Numbers	2	**E:** Side Control	#4-6
Green	TG3	Applications	3	**F:** Basic Grappling Positions	#4-6
Blue Stripe	TG4	Around the Dojang	3	**G:** Mount Escapes	#7-9
Blue	TG5	Sparring Match	4	**1:** Defense against Tackle **2:** Defense against Boxer	#7-9
Red Stripe	TG6	Stances	4	**3:** Clinch Attack **4:** Defense against Takedown	#10-12
Red	TG7	Kicks, Strikes and Blocks	5	**5:** Ground Defense against Striking **6:** Defense against Headlock	#13-15
Black Stripe	TG8	Body Parts and Directions	5	**7:** Throw from Clinch **8:** Leg Submissions	#16-18
Double Black Stripe	Choong Mo	All moves of TG1	5	**9:** Defense against Kick **10:** Wheel Throw Series	3 of own

Quick Grappling Summary

Grappling is just summarized. See Grappling chapter for full requirements (pg123). (Note that some grappling drills are rotated in After School Programs and may be different per belt.)

White to Yellow belt: Grap A and B
A: Falling Technique – Left, right, back and front. Don't hit your head or land on elbows or wrists.

B: Rolling Technique – Forwards and back on each shoulder. Can be done from kneeling. Make sure not to hit your head by putting it to the side when going backwards.

Yellow to High Yellow belt: Grap C and D
C: Standing Control: Swim ten times and then lift your partner by getting both underhooks.

D: Riding the back: Half circle to the right, half circle back, half circle to the left, half circle back, full circle to the right, full circle to the left..

High Yellow to Green belt: Grap E
E: Side Control: Go through positions 1-4.

Green to High Green belt: Grap F (*Never Ending*)
F: Basic Grappling Positions: Pass guard, mount, get back, let partner turn into guard.

High Green to Blue belt: Grap G
G: Mount Escapes: Both partners do shrimp and hip bump sweep, then one throws the legs to pass guard while the other sweeps. Finish with standing drill.

Blue to High Blue belt: Grap 1 and 2
  1. **Defense against a tackle.** Alex rushes at Bob to take him down. GUILLOTINE CHOKE, KIMURA LOCK, HIP BUMP SWEEP.

2. **Defense against a boxer**. Alex comes at Bob with several punches. Bob dodges until he finds a good punch and does DOUBLE LEG TAKEDOWN to the mount. BENT ARM BAR, ARM BAR.

High Blue to Red belt: Grap 3 and 4
3. **Clinch attack.** From the clinch, Bob gets one underhook and then does DUCK UNDER TAKEDOWN, CLOCK CHOKE TRIANGLE CHOKE.

4. **Defense against Takedown.** Alex shoots and then Bob defends by SPRAWLING, CROSS FACE and BACK RIDE, BACK CHOKE, ARM BAR from the back

Red to High Red belt: Grap 5 and 6
5. **Ground defense against striking.** Bob shoots and Alex defends by SPRAWLING, HALF DUMP, three knee strikes, SHRIMPS and puts in his guard. FRONT CHOKES, ARM BAR from the guard.

6. **Defense against headlock.** From headlock, trip backwards and kick over & take mount. When partner shrimps with hand on knee, trap the arm at 90 degrees and rolls to his back to apply KIMURA LOCK and then OMAPLATA.

High Red to Dbl Black Stripe Red belt: Grap 7 and 8
7. **Throw from clinch.** From the clinch, Bob takes down Alex with HEADLOCK THROW. Bob applies SIDE CHOKE, then kicks over to ARM BAR FROM #1 POSITION

8. **Leg Submissions**. From Alex's guard, Bob breaks the guard and goes for ANKLE LOCK, but Alex grabs the head and sits up to take the mount. Bob bridges and returns to Alex's guard and breaks it again, this time going for KNEE BAR. Bob lets go and then transitions to KNEE LOCK and finally takes Alex's back.

9. **Kick Defense.** Alex comes at Bob with a roundhouse kick, and Bob scoops under and does KICK DEFENSE TAKEDOWN. Alex holds Bob in the guard and goes for KIMURA LOCK, but Bob defends with REVERSE KIMURA LOCK. Bob then uses BEHIND THE BACK GUARD PASS to get to #1 position. From there, Alex tries to fend him off and Bob uses FAR SIDE ARM BAR.

10. **Wheel Throw Series.** Alex comes to push Bob and Bob counters with WHEEL THROW. Bob runs to put Alex in #4 position and applies KIMURA LOCK. Alex escapes by rolling backward to get the back mount. Alex tries to apply BACK CHOKE but Bob crosses Alex's legs and applies CROSSED ANKLE LOCK.

Quick One-Step Sparring Summary

* One-Step Sparring is just summarized. See the full requirements on each belt chapter.

Number	Description
1-Y	Block (left) & punch to face (Right), double punch to chest.
2-Y	Horse stance, knifehand block with left, knifehand strike to neck with right. Grab punching hand, step together, knifehand strike to neck with right. Sweep to ground with right leg, punch.
3-Y	Block with right, horsestance. Spin to cross stance, knifehand strike with left.
4-HY/G	Crescent kick with left, side kick with right.
5-HY/G	Block to the outside with left. (Two for one special – sweep and strike).
6-HY/G	(Matrix part 1) Move under punch. Ridgehand to sternum with right, backfist to temple with right. Shift long stance, ridgehand to temple with left.
7-HG/B	Block with right, spin, elbow, backfist, groin throw.
8-HG/B	(Matrix part 2) ridgehand with right, backfist, ridgehand with left.
9-HG/B	Block out to in with right. Foot-stomp, leg-pull, back kick to groin.
10-HB	(X-block series). X block, spin under arm (hold with right.) Elbow to spine, knee to tail bone, grab and throw goin.
11-HB	(Spin kicks) – start with left outside to inside crescent, spin hook, butterfly & step through.
12-HB	Jump front snap kicks
13-R	Left outside to inside knifehand block, spin arm and duck under to right tigers' mouth strike to neck.
14-R	(Bruce Lee) Block with left, punch, guillotine, back-heel kick.
15-R	(Super Slapper) Step left, knifehand block with right. Roundhouse, pull arm down, hook, roundhouse (right). Spinhook, roundhouse (left).

16-HR	Right inside to outside crescent, left step on knee, check off and right spin hook to face.
17-HR	Knifehand block with right to outside of punch. Scissors takedown. Knifehand strike to neck
18-HR	(The three submissions). Step with left, turning knifehand block with right, grab, key-lock and spin to takedown. Armbar. Pull into them sitting up, then triangle choke. Kick leg over into omoplata.

About the Authors

Master Bill Pottle joined the Korean Academy of Taekwondo as a white belt in 1992. He graduated from Overland High School and then earned his Bachelors and Masters degrees in Biological Engineering from Cornell University in Ithaca, NY where he lead the team to 5 consecutive Ivy/Northeast Collegiate Championship titles and served as the captain of the first league all-star team. He became the KAT Head Master in 2004 and has greatly expanded the school since them. He is also the author of several fantasy books which can be found at www.billpottle.com

Master Katie Pottle studied martial arts off and on many times throughout her life, but never found what she was looking for until she joined the Korean Academy while a student at Metro State University. She graduated from Metro State and earned her Bachelors degree in Biology. Later she earned her Masters Degree in Biological Science from the University of Nebraska. Katie is also the author of several young adult fantasy books which can be found at www.katiepottle.com

Together they balance running KAT, raising their family, and working with other businesses.

Made in the USA
Columbia, SC
07 January 2020